SAN FRANCISCO

A pocket guide to the city's best
cultural hangouts, shops, bars
and eateries

SAM TREZISE

Hardie Grant

TRAVEL

CONTENTS

INTRODUCTION

Beat poets, groovy people and tech-entrepreneurs alike – there's something about thinking differently that comes with the territory in San Francisco.

It's a city where you are free to be what you want and whoever you may be. It's the perfect backdrop for creativity and a judgement-free zone. Where ideas become a reality and where concepts become actualisations.

Although a city of constant change, San Francisco is a place that respects history, too. A place where some restaurants have had the same item on the menu since the '50s and the same person serving since the '70s. The nostalgia isn't just in the Victorian homes and the fog rolling in over the bay – it's in the attitude.

In one of my favourite diners (Tommy's Joynt) hangs a sign saying 'Welcome Stranger' and this, to me, is the most authentic image of San Francisco. More so than a Giants' baseball game, Janis Joplin or the Golden Gate Bridge.

When you're perched on a barstool, cosy in a leather booth, or on the rattling chair of a streetcar, chances are a local will tell you what they love about being a San Franciscan.

This book pays equal homage to the classics that make the Golden City so iconic and the current trends that make it so progressive. Together we'll explore the heart of Downtown, from the stalwart diners and dive bars to shopping at chic retailers and hidden cocktail haunts. I'll walk you around the famous wharves, guide you to the finest seafood on the coast and set you on course to the infamous Alcatraz Island. You'll see museums of art, science and one filled with coin-operated machines. We'll head to the best views the city has to offer – from the top of manmade Coit Tower to the naturally formed Twin Peaks.

When it's time to escape the hustle, we'll hit the road on field trips to the cultural hubs of Berkeley and Oakland, to California's acclaimed Napa Valley wine region and famed Yosemite National Park.

Sam

POCKET TOP PICKS

BEST CITY VIEWS

Twin Peaks, Haight & Golden Gate Park … 34

Mount Tamalpais, Santa Cruz & The Coast … 141

Coit Tower, Fisherman's Wharf, Russian Hill & Telegraph Hill … 17

Grace Cathedral, Nob Hill, Chinatown & Polk Street … 64

Lands End, Presidio, Outer Sunset & Lands End … 80

BEST SPECIALTY COFFEE

Sightglass (SFMOMA), South Beach, SOMA & Civic Center … 96

Ritual Coffee Roasters, Hayes Valley & Nopa, Napa Valley … 53 & 150

Four Barrel Coffee (The Mill), Hayes Valley & NOPA … 54

Blue Bottle Coffee (Ferry Building) … 2

Trouble Coffee, Presidio, Outer Sunset & Lands End … 82

BEST DINERS & DIVES

Spec's Twelve Adler Museum Cafe, Embarcadero, FIDI & North Beach … 9

Tempest, South Beach, SOMA & Civic Center … 101

Tommy's Joynt, Nob Hill, Chinatown & Polk Street … 65

Eddie's Cafe, Hayes Valley & NOPA … 50

Red's Java House, South Beach, SOMA & Civic Center … 98

TOP SEAFOOD SPOTS

Swan Oyster Depot, Nob Hill, Chinatown & Polk Street … 69

Scoma's, Fisherman's Wharf, Russian Hill & Telegraph Hill … 22

Tadich Grill, Embarcadero, FIDI & North Beach … 10

Bar Crudo, Hayes Valley & NOPA … 56

Hook Fish Co, Presidio, Outer Sunset & Lands End … 88

BEST BAKERIES

TOP RAINY DAY DESTINATIONS

BEST GREEN SPACES

INSPIRING ARCHITECTURE

SAN FRANCISCO OVERVIEW

SAUSALITO

MARIN
HEADLANDS

PRECINCTS

FIELD TRIPS

Golden
Gate

PRESID

GOLDEN
GATE PARK

INNER
SUNSET

GOLDEN
GATE
HEIGHTS

Pacific
Ocean

FORT
MCDOWELL

San
Francisco
Bay

ALCATRAZ
ISLAND

TREASURE
ISLAND

🚗 ⑪
🚆 ⑨
🚗 ⑫

②

⑤ ①

JAPANTOWN

DOWNTOWN

④ ⑦

MISSION
BAY

CASTRO

MISSION

San
Francisco
Bay

⑧

CENTRAL
WATERFRONT

SAN
FRANCISCO

HUNTERS
POINT

⬇ ⑩ 🚗

EMBARCADERO, FIDI & NORTH BEACH

Embarcadero – literally 'pier' in Spanish – is the primary marina-side boulevard Eastern Shoreline, a long waterside street running from Fisherman's Wharf (Pier 45) to the iconic clock tower of the Ferry Building (*see* p. 2). It's a great place for views of the bay, watching ships roll in and strolls along the coast. From Pier 33 you can visit the once formidable prison of Alcatraz (*see* p. 6), now a national park.

Nearby, in downtown, FIDI (financial district) is an area transforming daily, as skyscrapers continue to grow higher and denser each year – the most expensive commercial real estate in the country. It's an area filled with tech billboards and the infamous Californian start-up hustle and their lavish headquarters. Downtown is less about suits and briefcases and you're more likely to see folk sporting Microsoft backpacks and tattered band tees. After 6pm, FIDI comes alive with a cross-section of bars from elegant to brash, often operating within a stone's throw of each other.

A short Uber ride north, North Beach – or more particularly the southern quarter of Columbus Avenue – was once the home of San Francisco's Beatniks. It was a place where writers from the east and west coasts would come to explore progressive thinking and alternative ideas. You can still visit the cafes, bars and bookstores they spent time in, such as the iconic City Lights (*see* p. 7) and the Beat Museum (*see* p. 4).

Train (BART): Embarcadero, Montgomery St.

→ *Caffe Trieste*

SIGHTS
1. Ferry Building
2. Exploratorium
3. Beat Museum
4. Alcatraz

SHOPPING
5. City Lights

EATING & DRINKING
6. Caffe Trieste
7. Spec's Twelve Adler Museum Cafe
8. Tadich Grill

1 FERRY BUILDING

1 Ferry Building
415 983 8000
www.ferrybuildingmarket
place.com
Open Mon–Fri 10am–7pm,
Sat 8am–6pm, Sun 11am–5pm
(restaurant hours vary)
[MAP p. 175 E3]

You'll notice this building
from halfway down Market
Street because of its 75-metre
tall clock tower, its cohort of
skateboarders out the front
and ferries docked out the
back. You'll also find a polished
collection of iconic eateries,
such as **The Slanted Door**,
a Californian establishment
considered a home to modern
Vietnamese cuisine, or there's
more affordable take-away from
Out the Door. On the opposite
side of the building is famous
Gott's Roadside, where you'll
be 'pressed' to find a juicier
burger. With ocean views,
you'll find **Hog Island Oyster
Co**. that sells oysters sourced
just a few miles down the
coast. **Boulettes Larder** is
one of my favourite places to
enjoy a poached egg breakfast
and watch the gulls fly around
the Bay Bridge. There's also
a fairly upmarket but good
selection of shopping staples.
Blue Bottle Coffee with
their famous espresso, wine
merchants, **Book Passage**
bookshop, **Heath Ceramics**
and tourism information at
the kiosk.

POCKET TIP
Head to the flea markets
just outside the Ferry Building.
You'll find charms, necklaces,
handwoven goods and much
more. Out front there is also
a great farmers market on
Tuesdays, Thursdays and
Saturdays.

2 EXPLORATORIUM

Pier 15, The Embarcadero
415 528 4444
www.exploratorium.edu
Open Tues–Wed & Fri–Sun
10am–5pm, Thurs 10am–5pm
& 6–10pm
[MAP p. 175 D1]

POCKET TIP
On Thursday nights there's an adults-only experience with drinks, music and specialty film.

I was given no clues the first time I went to Exploratorium – I hadn't been on the website, and I hadn't heard much except that someone had given me the impression that it was kind of a museum designed for kids. I'm not sure if it's a reflection on my maturity, but I had the time of my life. It's an interactive landscape – surpassing the museum definition – filled with educational, quirky and intriguing exhibits. I stepped inside a tornado, turned life upside down in a room of curved mirrors, danced on a fog bridge and learned why buildings in San Francisco are made to move. I now know what stem cells, fruit flies and zebrafish look like under a microscope, and what can be built with 100,000 toothpicks! The highlight for me is the Tactile dome – an interactive excursion through total darkness – but it often requires reservations, so check the available time slots online. Entry to the Exploratorium for adults costs $29.95 and it's $19.95 for kids. I also recommend heading to the cafe and gift shop.

3 BEAT MUSEUM

540 Broadway
415 399 9626
www.kerouac.com
Open Mon–Sun 10am–7pm
[MAP p. 174 B2]

Alongside the Beat Generation of New York, San Francisco's North Beach was a pivotal part of this anti-conformist movement in the 1950s. Immerse yourself in the journeys of the young Beat poets (such as Jack Kerouac, William Burroughs and Allen Ginsberg), and learn how the careers of artists like The Beatles, Bob Dylan, Jim Morrison and many others were influenced. The museum is filled with original works, photographs and memorabilia displayed across two levels, including a projection room and the car that Cassidy and Kerouac used on their famous journey in *On the Road*. There's a bookshop with a discount tub (a literal bathtub), filled with fantastic secondhand $2 reads – perfect for the traveller looking to stock up on some Megabus reads. Museum entry costs $8 and organised tours of it and the North Beach area can be prepared for larger groups – the tour makes a great introduction to the area's history. Note too that the museum is undergoing a renovation (seismic retrofit) sometime in the near future. Check the website for information.

POCKET TIP
Jack Kerouac has an alley named after him wedged between City Lights (see p. 7) and Café Vesuvio, a mere 50-metres away from the museum.

4 ALCATRAZ

Alcatraz Island
415 981 7625
www.alcatrazcruises.com
[MAP p. 171 D1]

'The Rock' operated for 29 years as a federal prison. A supposedly inescapable island fortress, 36 prisoners attempted to escape; only 26 were caught alive and some say the remaining 10 succumbed to the icy waters of San Francisco Bay. Or did they? Head on over, on the less than 15-minute ferry ride from Pier 33 onboard the *Alcatraz* cruise vessel and make up your own mind. The island is no longer a prison but a national park, taking you into the heart of life in what was once the most secure prison in the world. You can walk around the cell blocks, learn the plans behind the escapes and stroll the magnificent gardens and parade grounds. Check the website or call to reserve your tickets, as there's different tours on offer – plus find out what you can and can't bring, what you should wear and how to catch the vessel over. Prices range from $40–$90. I undertook the **Night Tour**, which added another layer of chill to the place (as did the bay's cold winds). Both recorded and personally guided tours are available. If you like to dawdle, I'd recommend the recorded.

POCKET TIP
Did you know that Alcatraz is the home of the oldest operating lighthouse on the west coast of the United States?

5 CITY LIGHT∫

261 Columbus Ave
415 362 8193
www.citylights.com
Open Mon–Sun 10am–12am
[MAP p. 174 B2]

City Lights independent bookstore is a recognised Official Historic Landmark – the first time this accolade was granted to a business and not to a property in San Francisco. It's more like a bohemian library than a bookstore, and it provides a literary home for an independent publisher and readers alike, continually striving to be a hospice for independent thought and critical thinking. It has a rich history, founded in 1953, and has survived and grown through times of revolutionary ideas, such as the Beatniks, and provided a safe place for people to come together. Allen Ginsberg first read his famous *Howl* here. It started as a tiny triangular store on the corner of Columbus Avenue and now occupies three storeys filled with literature specialising in cultural movements, poetry and influential histories, as well as selected works published by City Lights itself. Flicking through the serpentine shelves might have you lost for hours, so reach out to the knowledgeable staff or attend one of the readings, launches or events.

7

EMBARCADERO, FIDI &
NORTH BEACH

6 CAFFE TRIESTE

601 Vallejo St
415 982 2605
www.coffee.caffetrieste.com
Open Mon–Sun 6.30am–11pm
[MAP p. 174 B2]

Papa Gianni was a Bay area Italian migrant that missed espresso so much, he simply had to be the first person to introduce it to the west coast and so, Caffe Trieste was born in 1956. The coffee shop was flocked to by the Italian community, and other restaurants fell in love with the Italian coffee concepts, too. This fabled cafe has seen generations of famed philosophers, poets and musicians ponder great ideas over a cup of delicious espresso and Italian biscotti and photos on the wall place Trieste in every period of modern San Franciscan history. Rumour has it that Francis Ford Coppola wrote much of *The Godfather* while sitting at the mosaic tables. Start a conversation with a local here and you'll quickly hear stories of them returning daily for 30-plus years. It's a great little spot for breakfast or lunch, or to enjoy a bagel, sandwich, slice of pie or a plate of antipasto.

POCKET TIP
Adjoined is a little retail store that sells all types of Italian coffee products, including Trieste's own blends for you to take home.

7 SPEC'S TWELVE ADLER MUSEUM CAFE

12 William Saroyan Pl
415 421 4112
Open Mon–Sun 4pm–2am
[MAP p. 174 B2]

Let's get this straight – this is not a museum (or at least not in the traditional sense) but a bar, although an absurdly cluttered one full of curious hoardings. Like the longshoremen, dockers and poets who have gone before, you'll discover a back bar, flag-clad ceiling and walls lined with maritime relics and oceanic oddities. I noted tribal masks, antique signs, ancient Buddha statues, lizard skin daggers and a carved walrus tusk – all dated, labelled and legered as if to proclaim: 'don't be fooled this is an actual museum!' The drinks selection is simple (house wines, a few draught beers and the staple spirits), the music is low, so naturally the conversation is good, the lighting is dim and the mood is pleasant. A solo punter can easily procure conversation with folks who've been drinking here since at least the early '70s. In fact, stories of Spec's have become such local lore that a documentary film is currently in production.

EMBARCADERO, FIDI &
NORTH BEACH

8 TADICH GRILL

240 California St
415 391 1849
www.tadichgrill.com
Open Mon–Sat 11am–9.30pm
[MAP p. 175 D3]

This seafood and steak restaurant is part of my history, San Francisco's history and United States' history. My history because I recall going with my father to get keepsakes of a bottle of housemade bloody mary mix and swizzle sticks. San Francisco's history because it's over 166 years old – you can see the many proprietors noted in the stairwell. And United States' history because it claims to be the third longest-running restaurant in the country. It will become part of your history, too, with the chefs and wait staff learning your name and how you like your steak cooked. Cosmopolitan salad or classics like Cioppino (fish stew), mesquite broiled salmon and shrimp salad come out of the kitchen hundreds of times a week. Dark wood panelling with large mirrors cover the walls and Art Deco brass light fixtures hang from the 15-foot ceiling (4 metres). Peak times can be busy but seating at the bar is usually up for grabs whilst you wait for a more intimate leather booth. It takes no reservations, proclaiming that 'regardless of fame and fortune, all are equal.'

FISHERMAN'S WHARF, RUSSIAN HILL & TELEGRAPH HILL

This north-eastern section of the coast is a popular traveller base, and I dare say even the most trendy of locals put down their pretension and bring their out-of-towners to Fisherman's Wharf.

The precinct has uncomplicated access to a range of activities, such as catching a cable car, strolling down iconic and steep Lombard Street (see p. 16) in Russian Hill or catching those breathtaking city views from Coit Tower (see p. 17) in Telegraph. You can try famed food, such as blowing on a bread bowl of smouldering chowder or making yourself sick inhaling a famous Ghirardelli sundae (see p. 20) in North Beach.

There's a generous dose of San Francisco nostalgia, such as Pier 39 (see p. 14) and Musée Mécanique (see p. 15) that embrace the charm of a 1950s coastal boardwalk fun zone. You can stock up on souvenirs, spot a sea lion, buy your tickets for out-of-town adventures or play on old pinball machines. The California coastline has a history of amusement parks and penny arcades – generations of fun-seekers have flocked to the water's edge in Santa Cruz, San Diego and, of course, San Francisco.

For me, I enjoy the great local seafood – places like Scoma's (see p. 22) that has been peddling local hauls for years.

Light rail (Muni metro): Embarcadero & Stockton St

→ *Aerial view of Lombard Street*

SIGHTS
1. Pier 39
2. Musée Mécanique
3. Lombard Street
4. Coit Tower

EATING
5. Boudin
6. Ghirardelli
7. Scoma's
8. Carmel Pizza Company

DRINKING
9. The Buena Vista

1 PIER 39

Pier 39, Embarcadero
www.pier39.com
Open Mon–Sun 10am–10pm
[MAP p. 173 E2]

There's no denying that this is maybe the most touristy location in San Francisco, but this marina-style family friendly eating and shopping destination has something for everyone. It's the kind of place that locals take people from out of town. Dine at America's favourite novelty food chains like **Hard Rock Café** and **Bubba Gump Shrimp Co.** or grab something more portable from the kiosks: cotton candy, churros, corn dogs – carnival foods galore. And don't miss **Boudin** bakery (*see* p. 18). It's not the cheapest place for souvenirs (that would be Chinatown a few blocks away), but it certainly has the most extensive collection of Warriors jerseys, Alcatraz hats, Cal sweatshirts and Twin Peaks (*see* p. 34) snow globes. The **Candy Baron** stocks every American sweet your friends have asked you to bring home. The rest of the shops are a slightly bizarre collection – a store catering exclusively to the left-handed and an outfitter stocking only socks (both right and left). Hang out amongst the street performers, see sea lions lazing on pontoons and if you're travelling with young children, there's a two-storey carousel.

POCKET TIP

Catch the Historic F-Market Streetcar from Embarcadero to the end of the wharf for a great view (on a clear day) of the Golden Gate Bridge, Angel Island, Alcatraz (*see* p. 6) and the Bay Bridge.

2 MUSÉE MÉCANIQUE

Pier 45, Fisherman's Wharf
415 346 2000
www.museemecaniquesf.com
Open Mon–Sun 10am–8pm
[MAP p. 172 C2]

Musée Mécanique is a boardwalk nostalgic penny arcade without the big carnival rides and the hordes of people. Whether you are 18 or 80, there is something in here that will remind you of your youth. It's at the back of Pier 45, tucked in between seafood restaurants and a World War II submarine (well worth a look, too), and offers 300 coin-operated machines/exhibits. The oldest is a praxinoscope dating back to 1886, the more recent include Time Crisis and Cruising USA from the noughties. You'll hear the melodies of coin-operated pianos and the constant flipping of pinball machines. Load up on quarters and test your love life on a turn-of-the-century-old Kiss-o-meter, or get your palm read by a robotic fortune teller. Take a Polaroid photo in a booth or challenge someone to a game of Space Invaders. San Francisco's famous Playland used to lay at Sutro Baths (see p. 80) and is where much of this collection comes from, although there are machines that have crossed every ocean to get here, too.

POCKET TIP

Edward Zelinsky founded Musée Mécanique, starting his collection when he was 11, repairing machines himself. Although Ed has passed, his family and a few other special individuals keep the museum alive.

15

3 LOMBARD STREET

**Between Hyde & Leavenworth
Streets**
[MAP p. 172 B4]

Locally described as the
'most crooked street in the
world', and one of the most
beautiful and iconic, Lombard
Street is a particularly windy
and steep segment, even by
San Francisco standards.
This particular portion of the
residential street stretches
approximately 180 metres
(590 feet) between Hyde and
Leavenworth Streets, and offers
a garden cascading down the
centre of it and spectacular
views of Coit Tower (*see*
p. 17), the Bay Bridge and
even Misión San Francisco de
Asís (*see* p. 109). The curving
street was originally designed
to slow traffic and minimise
the naturally staggering
27 per cent incline that the
automobiles of 1922 certainly
would have struggled with.
You can actually still drive
down part of it, although I
wouldn't recommend it, as
queues can often take up to
half an hour. I recommend
parking nearby or attempting
the calve-burning hike to Hyde
Street (at the top) from the
pier side and walking down,
as the surrounding Victorian
mansions are pristine and the
gardens are charming. The
best photograph of the street
is taken from the bottom.

4 COIT TOWER

1 Telegraph Hill Blvd
Open Mon–Sun 10am–5pm
[MAP p. 173 F4]

It wouldn't be the same city without the steep hills, and if you can manage a relatively exhausting hike through Pioneer Park, past Victorian homes and steep driveways (or catch the #39 MUNI bus), you'll be rewarded with spectacular views. Built during the Great Depression in 1932 in Art Deco style, this memorial tower is set on land bequeathed by San Francisco's legendary patroness of firefighters, Lillie Hitchcock Coit. The tower and surrounding park commemorate the city's pioneers. After walking the marble steps and through the entrance, you'll see social-realism-style murals, painted by 25 artists, that represent the archetype founding classes of the city. The lift takes up to 2500 people a day (but there are stairs at the top), and it can be a long wait on weekends, so time your visit for weekdays if you can. Some 64 metres (210 feet) higher, you can check out the view from every window, looking over different parts of the city. The coolest thing about the tower is the secret stairs. Go on a clear and dry day for maximum visibility and to avoid getting wet through the open roof. The entry fee is $9.

5 BOUDIN

Baker's Hall
160 Jefferson Street
Bakery & Bakers Hall
415 928 1849
Bistro Boudin 415 351 5561
boudinbakery.com/boudin-at-
the-wharf
Bakery & Bakers Hall Open
Mon–Sun 8am–9pm
Bistro Boudin Open Mon–Sun
11.30am–10pm
[MAP p. 172 C2]

If you haven't had a bread bowl brimming with creamy clam chowder, then you're not truly experiencing this city. Whilst there are a hundred places in the area that make it, this is my recommended place to go. Rolling around since 1849, Boudin still uses the same yeast culture (mother strain) it developed 150 years back. With live baking on view and the insightful **Bakery Museum** (see pocket tip), you're in for a ride. You can sample oven-fresh dough and experience the bakers' process from start to finish through the 9 metre (30 foot) observation window. Plus you get the experience of getting the iconic bread bowl of chowder for under a tenner. For those looking for a more formal visit, there's a fantastic restaurant **Bistro Boudin**, upstairs, serving ceviche, crab cakes, damn good fish tacos and naturally, oysters. There's also a marketplace and gift shop, so you can stock up on baked or picnic-perfect foods.

SANDWICH ROLL $2.49

DUTCH CRUNCH $1.59

JALAPENO CHEDDAR ROLL $4.29

BABY TEDDY BEAR $5.29

BABY TURTLE $5.29

MINING CAMP BREAD $10.49

POCKET TIP
The Bakers Hall and
Bakery Museum run tours
daily and there's a range
of different options, so
check its website if you
have a serious appetite
for baked goods.

6 GHIRARDELLI

900 North Point St
415 474 3938
www.ghirardellisq.com
Open Sun–Thurs 9am–11pm,
Fri–Sat 9am–12am
[MAP p. 172 A3]

An Italian born, Peru-raised
chocolatier moves to the Bay
Area during the Californian
gold rush, eventually opening
a charming store on the corner
of Broadway and Battery in
1850, and as fast as you can say
'American's love chocolate',
a series of factories and
production houses popped up
around the city. A few were
located on what we now know
as Ghirardelli Square, where
you can head to encounter
Ghirardelli's world-famous fudge
and chocolate at its flagship
store. Fill your backpack with
Ghirardelli's little squares of
bliss, and they'll hardly last the
Uber ride home. My personal
affliction is the salted caramel
dark. For more chocolate fun,
join the queue to the fudgery
and order up one of the (quite
large and very shareable)
sundaes – take a peek at the
functional chocolate making
going on all around you. To
avoid the queue, you can get
your sundae to go from another
Ghirardelli store, from the corner
of Larkin Street and North Point
Street just around the corner!

POCKET TIP

Ghirardelli Square offers a range of retailers, dining and panoramic vistas of the bay. There's The Cheese School of San Francisco for the more savoury characters and San Francisco Brewing Co. for a pint or two.

7 SCOMA'S

1965 Al Scoma Way
415 771 4383
www.scomas.com
Open Mon–Thurs 12pm–9pm,
Fri & Sun 11.30am–9.30pm,
Sat 11.30am–9.30pm
[MAP p. 172 B2]

Scoma's is a bonafide boat to table (pier to plate) eatery and has been so since 1965. In fact, boats can cruise right up to the restaurant and drop off their catch. What started as a small coffee shop that served burgers and coffee – fast forward 50 years and it's still family owned, and a restaurant that the city has named the street after. The motto is: Fresh, Local, Organic, Seasonal and Sustainable. After kicking your meal off with Californian beers, try the world-famous Lazy Man's Cioppino. Cioppino is an Italian San Francisco dish – essentially a fish stew filled with everything delicious that can be plucked out of the ocean. If you're looking for something a bit lighter, the shrimp louie salad, dungeness crab cocktail and the smoked salmon bruschetta are great ways to start an evening. The drinks menu is filled with Californian whites to pair with your seafood. If you want the experience without the price tag, lunch is a great option. You'll get Anchor beer-battered fish and chips for under $20.

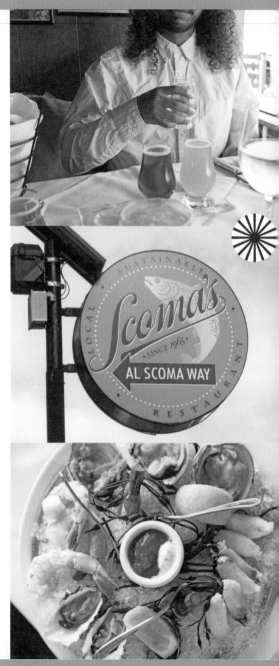

8 CARMEL PIZZA COMPANY

2826 Jones St
415 676 1185
www.carmelpizzaco.com
Open Mon–Tues & Thurs
11.30am–3.30pm & 5–8pm,
Wed & Fri 11.30am–8pm,
Sat 12pm–8pm, Sun 12pm–
6.30pm
[MAP p. 172 C2]

Buried amongst the mounds
of restaurants cracking
open crab legs and stirring
up bowls of Cioppino (fish
stew), sits an unsuspecting
Neapolitan-style wood-oven
pizzeria. Typically, local pizza
offerings include the likes of
Chicago deep dish, Detroit
square-pan, taco toppings or
Thai flavours (eek!), but here
every pizza that comes out of
the wood-oven has a thin and
crispy crust. Bases are smeared
with zesty cherry plum tomato
sauce, olive oil and fresh fior di
latte mozzarella. Although all
simplistic, the flavour combos
are thoughtful and considerate
of tradition. Ingredients
like sweet Italian sausage,
prosciutto crudo di parma,
applewood-smoked ham and
marinated artichoke are all
scattered around the menu.
The modest vine-covered
courtyard seating is pleasant
and relaxing and the ordering
process is no fuss. Service is
quick, head up to the counter
and let them know what
you want.

23

9 THE BUENA VISTA

2765 Hyde St
415 474 5044
www.thebuenavista.com
Open Mon–Sat 9am–2am,
Sun 8am–2am
[MAP p. 172 B3]

On a corner of Hyde Street, across from where the cable cars run past, sits a diner that's been famous for serving its Irish Coffee since 1916. It's the city's longest continually running business and the home of the original Irish Coffee in the United States. This coffee is so famous they serve upwards of 2000 of them a day and used 184,350 litres (48,700 gallons) of Tullamore whiskey just last year. The coffee's secret is 48-hour aged buttery cream. If Irish coffee isn't quite your poison then the house-made Bloody Mary's a great prospect. As the name suggests, there's a sweeping marina view, while you sit amongst the charming (not divey) character of an authentic American-style Irish pub. You'll be served by veteran waiters that love the place so much they have been clocking in on average for 25 years. The menu is hearty with solid portions of household favourites, like the cable car meatloaf and dungeness crab salad. For breakfast, try the BV combo or crispy corn beef hash.

POCKET TIP
Make your way to
The Buena Vista
on the cable car 1
with a single ride
for $7.

HAIGHT & GOLDEN GATE PARK

When you tell someone over 60 you're going to San Francisco, they'll likely tell you to 'put a flower in your hair' or 'say hi to Wavy Gravy for me'. The San Francisco they are alluding to, from the 1960s, lives on (in some form) in Haight-Ashbury. Haight (the suburb) and Ashbury (the major cross street) represented all things flower power and groovy in a time of change, rebellion and social evolution. These days, you'll more likely see punks and street kids, however, there is still an aroma of the free life in the air. You'll still find storefronts painted in rainbow selling tie-dye clothes, warehouse-sized record stores and thrift stores filled with curated rare finds. Then there's a series of seedy smoke shops, Tibetan marketplaces and fringe spirituality stores. Several cool-kid Californian brands have made Haight their headquarters, too.

Along the Haight Street strip, you're never far from a burger, pizza or a cold can of beer. I'd suggest checking in at one of the haunts that famous flower children like Hendrix and Ginsberg frequented. Consider Zam Zam (see p. 39) or Cha Cha Cha (see p. 40), all still with a pre-hippie-dom vibe.

At the eastern end of Haight Street, you'll find the entrance to Golden Gate Park, which sprawls across five suburbs, culminating at Ocean Beach – it's significantly larger than New York's Central Park and even has bison populating it. Here you'll find the Botanical Garden (see p. 28), the Japanese Tea Garden (see p. 30), the de Young Museum (see p. 32) and the California Academy of Sciences (see p. 33).

Light rail (Muni metro): Carl & Cole St

→ Victorian houses in the Haight district

SIGHTS
1. San Francisco Botanical Garden
2. Japanese Tea Garden
3. de Young Museum
4. California Academy of Sciences
5. Twin Peaks

SHOPPING
6. Loved to Death
7. Amoeba Records
8. Wasteland

EATING & DRINKING
9. Zam Zam
10. Cha Cha Cha

1 SAN FRANCISCO BOTANICAL GARDEN

1199 9th Ave
www.sfbg.org
Open Mon–Sun 7.30am–5pm
[MAP p. 184 A3]

Pull out your picnic and sprawl out on the meadow under great cypress (folks have been doing so since the 1800s) amongst 55 blooming acres of inner-city respite in the heart of Golden Gate Park – great for shaking off jet lag. Or instead, find a more secluded patch deeper in for a bit of privacy. It's $9 admission for travellers, but if you're a local you'll enter for free. Plant-wise, there's an array of seasonal highlights representing just about every single botanical zone. From an Indian natural cloud forest to delicately cultivated rare species of winter magnolias, and amongst the 8500 different types of uniques, there's going to be a bloom for you. You can easily spend a few hour here, but if you only have time to pick a few quick stops, I'd recommend the **Garden of Fragrance** – it's like an all-natural scratch-and-sniff book in the form of a garden bed, showing-off clever aromatic plants. And, don't leave without seeing the famous 100+ year-old Californian redwoods.

POCKET TIP
If you're going to do this right, grab a picnic from Whole Foods Market just at the end of Haight Street before you enter Golden Gate Park.

2 JAPANESE TEA GARDEN

75 Hagiwara Tea Garden Dr
415 752 1171
www.japaneseteagardensf.com
Open Mon–Sun 9am–4.45pm
[MAP p. 184 A2]

Just around the corner from the Botanical Garden (see p. 28), you can be transported to rural Japan. Meander the delicate grounds filled with epic pagodas, shrines and pristine hedges. Cross trickling streams and ponds filled with Koi and coins, storing the wishes of travellers past. Or why not find your balance in the karesansui (Japanese stone garden). I was genuinely surprised as to how it all fits in the space I saw from the outside. Enjoy a relaxing glass of sencha, oolong or matcha – made authentically – and slurp up a quick bowl of udon noodles in the irori (sunken hearth) overlooking a tranquil pond surrounded by communal seating in a traditional Japanese style. You pay to enter but it's worth it, at $6 for adult residents and $9 for non-residents.

POCKET TIP
There's a Chinese fortune cookie factory to visit in Chinatown (see p. 62), but legend has it that this is the birthplace of the style of fortune cookie we all crack open today!

3 DE YOUNG MUSEUM

50 Hagiwara Tea Garden Dr
415 750 3600
deyoung.famsf.org
Open Tues–Sun 9.30am–5.15pm
[MAP p.184 B2]

The de Young was founded in 1895 and built in an epic Egyptian revival style, with the massive **Hamon Observation Tower** spiralling up out of it. The museum houses exhibitions from greats like Monet, Turner and Georgia O'Keefe and is located in the most colossally decorated, wide-opened grandiose passage of Golden Gate Park opposite the **California Academy of Sciences** (*see* p. 33). For me, the joy of the de Young is the spread of historic artefacts and contemporary art. You'll wander past colossal cracked stones, a three-piece ball gown and a work created from the charcoal of a church destroyed by arson. The American art collection shows works from the 17th century to present day and is a great opportunity to see the progression and history of creativity within the United States. The museum has a packed calendar of one-off screenings and events, so be sure to check its website. Tickets cost $15 and include same-day general admission to the **Legion of Honor** museum.

POCKET TIP

The highlight for me is the observation tower – head on up and see a sprawling panoramic view of the city and Golden Gate Park from inside the museum.

4 CALIFORNIA ACADEMY OF SCIENCES

55 Music Concourse Dr
415 379 8000
www.calacademy.org
Open Mon–Sat 9.30am–5pm,
Sun 11am–5pm
[MAP p. 184 B2]

Explore the universe of learned sciences within an academy that was formed a mere three years after the formation of the United States. Check the viewing times at the planetarium as a priority pit-stop – there's a range of demonstrations each day. Next stop, walk the levels of the four-story rainforest enclosure filled with ferns, frogs, butterflies and birds of every conceivable shape, size, colour and pattern. Below deck you'll head to the aquarium, encountering the joys of a Filipino coral reef, see fish communicating with dotted light luminescence, play with starfish in the tide pool and contemplate the motions of a South Australian leafy sea dragon. Last stop is the green roof, a living structure representing the major hills of San Francisco – you can head up there via the lift but the perfect place to view is from the observation deck of the **de Young museum** (*see* p. 32), directly across the way. Entrance to the academy costs $35.95.

5 TWIN PEAKS

501 Twin Peaks Blvd
sfrecpark.org/destination/twin-peaks
Open Mon–Sun 5am–12am
[MAP p. 170 C4]

Offering panoramic city views, Twin Peaks are set in a 60-acre recreation park, forming on a point almost 282 metres (922 feet) above sea-level. Here you can see the fog rolling in over the Pacific Ocean, tankers pulling into the port, and you can photograph every significant San Francisco landmark in one sitting. On a clear day, you'll see as far as Cobb Mountain and the Santa Clara Valley. Put aside an hour or so to walk to the top of both peaks, which are named **Eureka** to the north and **Noe** to the south. The site's elevation makes it a prime position for radio transmitters, including the famous **Sutro Tower**. If the peaks appear too treacherous, there is a viewing platform with binoculars signposted from the carpark. Naturally, sunset and sunrise are the best times for photographs, but this area has been known for theft and other criminal activity in the later evening, so stay safe! To my knowledge there is no link with the same name TV show, so if you were hoping for a Lynch'esque murder mystery tour, you've come to the wrong place!

POCKET TIP
There is no public transport to the peaks, but the 37 Corbett MUNI bus will pitch you a short walk away. The most hassle-free and convenient way to get there is by rental car or rideshare.

6 LOVED TO DEATH

1681 Haight St
415 551 1036
www.lovedtodeath.com
Open Wed–Mon 12pm–7pm
[MAP p. 185 F2]

Loved to Death is dedicated to the promotion of positive witchcraft and magic. Peculiarities overflow from this little shopfront, which was set up by a coven of local 'spiritualists' ten years ago, today the owner is the only one that remains. You'll see taxidermy animals wearing hats – the owner sees creative reuse. It's your one-stop-shop for ritual candles for every situation, even if it's just making an apartment smell better. Enchanted soaps made by a local witch can work miracles, including taming traveller's odours! Considered getting into a bit of witchcraft? The place makes their own branded 'starter kit' for spells and potions. Or perhaps you've wanted to play your hand at tarot? The collections are quite large and a range of manuals and textbooks for tarot and other practices are available. My favourites items are the collection of perfumes made by The Horror Scene, one of which is designed exclusively for Loved to Death.

7 AMOEBA RECORDS

1855 Haight St
415 831 1200
www.amoeba.com
Open Mon–Sun 11am–8pm
[MAP p. 185 E3]

Occupying an old bowling alley on the eastern edge of Golden Gate Park, this massive record store boasts 100,000-plus titles across vinyl, video and CD. Not the oldest record store on the strip but undeniably the largest, this analogue paradise stands tall, busy as ever in a time of aggressive digital takeover. The trio of Amoeba stores (the others are in Hollywood and Downtown Berkeley) have a somewhat cultish status amongst musicians and fans alike. Encompassing every conceivable genre and with CDs as low as $1, this is the ideal spot to stock up for your road trip up the Pacific Northwest. You'll find an entire room dedicated to film and the largest collection of tees, embroidered patches, enamel pins and gig posters. Literature, zines and even musically themed ritual candles are on offer. If you're drawn to the local scene, a huge effort goes into Bay Area music, promoting neighbourhood shows (even having them in store), and the wider outreach of sales supports rainforests and indigenous communities.

POCKET TIP
Haight-Ashbury's home to the house of Jimi Hendrix and Hippie Hill in Golden Gate Park, a magical place that once attracted the likes of Janis Joplin and the Grateful Dead.

8 WA/TELAND

1660 Haight St
415 863 3150
www.shopwasteland.com
Open Mon–Sat 11am–8pm,
Sun 11am–7pm
[MAP p. 185 F2]

Located in what's rumoured to have once been a vintage theatre that focused on raunchy films, this vintage store combines Haight-Ashbury's nostalgia, San Francisco's passion for recycling and a local obsession with progressive fashion. For over 30 years this second-hand paradise has seen curated, clean and affordable fashion pass through its doors. Every Californian fashion hound has a story or two of their great label finds amongst the Wasteland racks – from Marc Jacobs and Vivienne Westwood to Prada. You'll be hard-pressed to click-clack through these racks without finding something for you, while the ambience is set by low-key soft rock playing in the background. You'll find the perfect clash of flared pants, '90s tracksuits, Doc Marten boots and hexagon-rimmed glasses. If you prefer to trade rather than buy, you can simply swap some of your traveller clothing for something new to you.

9 ZAM ZAM

1633 Haight St
415 861 2545
Open Mon–Fri 3pm–2am,
Sat–Sun 1pm–2am
[MAP p. 185 F2]

Like just about everything on this strip, there's a history here, and Zam Zam's got a lot from 1941 still out on display. From the Persian mural on the rear wall to the cash register, the jukebox and the photos adorning the walls. Famously known for their martinis and, well, a classist bar owner that was known for kicking anyone out who didn't order a martini – today you can order whatever you want. And for $6 during happy hour ($8 normally), why wouldn't you? Sit at the polished front bar taking in the sounds of smooth jazz, like Billie Holiday and Dave Brubeck, and get lost amongst the paisley wallpaper, listening to the idle chatter of people that sound like they've known each other their entire lives. Conversely, head to the back for a more intimate lamp-lit setting with Parisian woven chairs. Happy hour is from 3–6pm and this is a bar you can feel comfortable in coming to alone.

39

10 CHA CHA CHA

1801 Haight St
415 386 7670
chachachasf.com
Open Mon–Thurs & Sun
11.30am–11pm, Fri–Sat
11.30am–11.30pm
[MAP p. 185 E3]

Within a few months of Cha Cha Cha's opening in the mid '70s, there was a line forming down the street all the way to Golden Gate Park. The Santeria-themed decor alone is worth the visit – carved Tahitian masks, colourful Guadalupe statues, photos of ancient hippies, crystal balls and indoor plants. Rest your palms on the vibrant tablecloth as you await an extraordinary fusion of Cuban, Cajun and Spanish cuisine – born from a string of different owners with different backgrounds. If you're looking for food recommendations and keen on something really unique, the vieja ropa (shredded steak) sided with slaw and caramelised potatoes really hits the spot. The mixta (kind of like a seafood paella) is also a house favourite. If you're down for a group graze, there's a tapas menu built to share; I insist that you order the Cajun shrimp, and if you're wanting to make it quick and filling, the cubanos (sandwiches) are on point. There might be a queue but it will move fast and the space is large.

HAYE/ VALLEY & NOPA

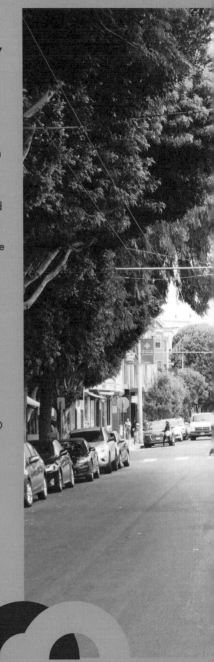

Part of the Western Addition – a collection of famous small neighborhoods – the tree-lined Hayes streets are filled with a savvy collection of shopping boutiques, really decent bars and a solid collection of renowned eateries. Hayes feels really pleasant, strolling through Patricia's Green (the central green space) and shopping in the markets on the weekend. The terrace houses are well kept and the people seem to smile a little bit more than everywhere else; there's a real community vibe. Public parks are all over this area, from Alamo Square to Waller Street, so there's places everywhere where you can sit down and sprawl on the grass.

Also part of the Western Addition but further west towards Golden Gate Park, you'll find NOPA (north of Panhandle) is filled with classic Victorian homes, including the famous Painted Ladies (see p. 44). The cafes are on point and the restaurants have all earned booking requirements. Walking into shops like Welcome Stranger (see p. 49) and TOPO Designs (see p. 48), the staff seem to have a genuine interest in how your day is going, making you feel like a local.

Japantown 'Nihonmachi' in Japanese, see p. 46) is only really a collection of a few blocks but, it can honestly feel like you're dining, shopping and walking around in Japan – from ramen joints to Japanese groceries. This was one of several Japanese districts but has over time become the largest in the United States.

Train (BART): Civic Center

↪ *Strolling down Hayes Street*

SIGHTS
1. Painted Ladies & Alamo Square

SHOPPING
2. Japantown
3. TOPO Designs
4. Welcome Stranger

EATING
5. Eddie's Cafe
6. NOPA
7. Zuni Cafe
8. The Mill
9. Bar Crudo

DRINKING
10. Smuggler's Cove
11. Toronado

1 PAINTED LADIE/ & ALAMO /QUARE

Steiner St & Hayes St
[MAP p. 180 C2]

This residential neighbourhood and park has debatably the most photographed site in the city: the Painted Ladies – a cluster of well-preserved Victorian houses. Chances are that you've seen them in the opening scene of a movie set in San Francisco or on Instagram. But why are these houses, out of the 48,000 Victorian houses in San Francisco, so famous? Many of these traditionally grey houses were colourfully transformed in the '60s, and they have become quintessential of the contrast that lives in San Francisco's past and present. The grassy parks are also a fantastic place to rest your legs, have a toilet stop and if you've got little ones, visit the playgrounds. If the army of tripods, selfie sticks and dudes selling polaroids is killing your vibe, stroll up the hill a bit – to the south, you'll spot Sutro Tower and an equally engaging set of well ornately painted well-decorated homes that I actually think are cooler!

POCKET TIP

Standing in Alamo Park opposite, you can see the Transamerica Pyramid, Union Square (*see* p. 92) and Civic Center. As the fog rises and lights flicker in the distance, it looks like fireflies hovering over the bay.

2 JAPANTOWN

Between Pine St & Geary Blvd
[MAP p. 182 B4]

The Japanese population in San Francisco ranks fourth by percentage in the nation. Japantown, nihonmachi in Japanese or J-town to locals, is the major of a few small Japanese centres in San Francisco. The area stretches approximately six blocks, bordered on the north by Pine Street and to the south by Geary Boulevard. The **Peace Pagoda** sits in the centre, seen from blocks away, and surrounding it you'll find a series of underground **shopping malls** selling trinkets, nifty homewares and Japanese literature. I'd particularly advise checking out **Kinokuniya** bookstore. Pick up your Japanese snacks, instant ramen and sake at one of the local grocers. There's also an abundance of ramen, sushi, macha ice-cream and other traditional Japanese eateries. All in a style that many Japanese compare to the Ginza precinct in Tokyo.

3 TOPO DE∫IGN∫

645 Divisadero St
415 525 3749
www.topodesigns.com
Open Mon–Sat 10am–7pm,
Sun 10am–6pm
[MAP p. 180 A3]

Bridging that often obvious gap between goofy camping design and streetwear, TOPO sports a signature range of products fit for walking into a Nob Hill coffee shop and up a trailhead in Tahoe. The brand's got a reputation for American made high-quality wares, vibrant colours and out-of-the-box designs. If you're mid-trip and need to replace that rucksack or about to kick off that round-the-world trip and are in need of a quick dry jacket or polar fleece, TOPO has you sorted with lightweight, high-tech travel apparel that's well worth the extra few pennies. Hailing from Denver and Fort Collins, there's five stores in the United States, but this is the only one in California. While you're there, you might like a quick chat with the staff, as they're a small tight-knit group that prove that TOPO's a real community – many of the store staff are even used as models in the photo shoots.

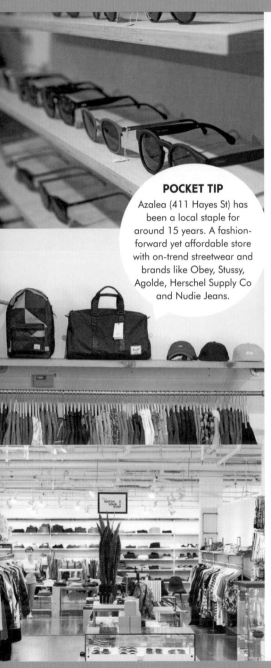

4 WELCOME STRANGER

460 Gough St
415 864 2079
www.welcomestranger.com
Open Mon–Sun 11am–7pm
[MAP p. 178 A3, 181 F2]

Welcome Stranger's a multi-brand retailer that focuses on shopping as an experience. Showcasing brands like Air, Carhartt, Barber and Topo and a series of interesting loot like lifestyle gear, such as candles, ceramic flasks, pipes, bongs and the very cool Komono sunglasses. It's a collection of brands for the dude that wants to look like he's done a great job pulling things out of his wardrobe but doesn't want to look as if he's spent too long in front of the mirror. Sundays at Welcome Stranger include beer tasting, pop-ups partnering with local vintage stores and workshops on skills, such as painting denim – all open to the public.

POCKET TIP

Azalea (411 Hayes St) has been a local staple for around 15 years. A fashion-forward yet affordable store with on-trend streetwear and brands like Obey, Stussy, Agolde, Herschel Supply Co and Nudie Jeans.

5 EDDIE'S CAFE

800 Divisadero St
415 563 9780
Open Mon–Sun 7.30am–
3.30pm
[MAP p. 180 A2]

Eddie's is a small place with a big heart and owners with personality that can only be rivalled by the decor itself. A place so comfortable the mayor's been known to pop in for his scramble and griddle stack. As kids finish their breakfast and step out the door, the server, whom I presume is also the owner, walks over to hand them a sweet as she wipes their faces with a napkin. Homemade bobbleheads, novelty mugs, and a flier for jazz piano lessons hang on the wall next to a blossoming orchid. Worn vinyl booth seating surrounds tables covered edge-to-edge with plates of humble chow. Join the morning patrons for a full breakfast of omelettes, hash, sausage, thick-cut bacon and homemade biscuits. The 1974 menu hanging on the wall is like a spot-the-difference challenge with the current one – the prices have changed a bit, but honestly not much. There's still a payphone on the wall that's picked up continually from orders being called in, so Eddie's must be just as good on the go!

6 NOPA

560 Divisadero St
415 864 8643
www.nopasf.com
Open Mon–Thurs 5pm–12am,
Fri 5pm–1am, Sat 10.30am–
1am, Sun 10.30am–12am
[MAP p. 180 A3]

The perfect gathering place (if you can get a table), NOPA's the place you can impress both your mother-in-law and a group of trendy friends with obscure dietary requirements. Specialising in organic wood-fired cuisine, it prides itself on chef collaborations that bring weekly innovations to the table. Check it out as each menu is actually dated. Changing menus aside, there are some flagship dishes you'll always find available. We're talking pork chops with sherry onions, nine-hour cooked bolognaise and a wood-grilled burger that's hit iconic status. It's loosely upmarket American diner fare that's rebelling a bit. Book ahead, but while you await your table, you can get going on the liquor-forward cocktail list at a communal table. My favourite place to sit is up on the mezzanine level, watching the bustle of the restaurant, the bar and the kitchen. While you're there, you can view the murals telling a story of the businesses that have made NOPA what it is today.

7 ZUNI CAFE

1658 Market St
415 552 2522
zunicafe.com
Open Mon–Thurs 11.30am–
11pm, Fri–Sat 11.30am–12am,
Sun 11am–11pm
[MAP p.181 F3]

Budget warning – this is not
the place for the traveller
saving up for a ticket home,
although I have a plan to get
you through this experience
the more affordable way.
Waiters wearing waistcoats
carrying silver trays and
operatic music chirping
certainly makes you aware
you're in a classy place, but
not trying-too-hard classy –
it's classic classy. This spot
has been known by almost
every San Franciscan and has
been in the food reviews for
over 40 years. Try the classic
Zuni burger with shoestring
fries (and they'll happily cut
it in half). However, the must-
do experience is the brick
oven-roasted chicken for two,
served with warm bread salad
and mustard greens. This is
not for the diner in a rush or
with a plane to catch – it can
take up to an hour to prepare,
so you might need a bottle
of Napa chardonnay and an
interesting conversation lined
up while you wait. For some
more express favourites – the
Zuni caesar salad and the
mesquite-grilled options, such
as local king salmon, are often
travelled far for.

POCKET TIP
Ready for a coffee pick-
me-up? Head to San
Francisco's famous Ritual
Coffee Roasters (432b
Octavia St), opposite
Patricia's Green.

8 THE MILL

736 Divisadero St
415 345 1953
www.themillsf.com
Open Mon 7am–6pm, Tues–Sat
7am–9pm, Sun 7am–7pm
[MAP p. 180 A2]

This is the story of a baker and
roaster who came together
to create the perfect way to
kickstart your San Francisco
morning. Josey the baker has
the perfect Italian oven for
making the type of doughy,
zingy morning loaf that the
well-bred San Franciscan loves
to coat in freshly churned butter.
She also makes the delicate
pastries that get you to set your
alarm five minutes earlier. One
of the veterans of the Bay Area
third-wave coffee movement:
Four Barrel Coffee has been
roasting beans a short bike ride
away in Mission for a decade.
Here at The Mill, the food and
coffee combine to make the
perfect team. Bon Iver strums
in the background as you
enjoy your delicious pistachio
and blackberry twice-baked
croissant or avocado toast and
that perfect choice of single
origin that you've selected from
the 12 on offer. Around you,
people have made this space an
office, a living room and a place
for friends – here you'll really
feel like a local. There's plenty of
bean options and lovely loaves to
take home, too!

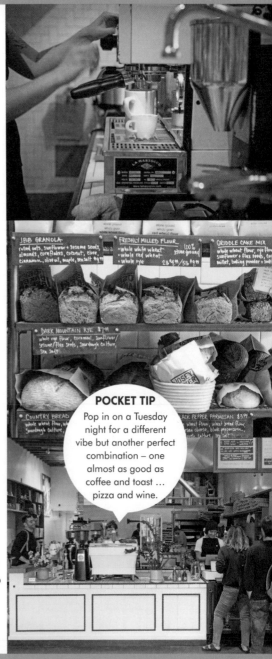

POCKET TIP
Pop in on a Tuesday
night for a different
vibe but another perfect
combination – one
almost as good as
coffee and toast …
pizza and wine.

9 BAR CRUDO

655 Divisadero St
415 409 0679
www.barcrudo.com
Open Tues–Thurs & Sun
5–10pm, Fri–Sat 5–11pm
[MAP p.180 A2]

For me, this is seafood done right – a series of perfectly fashioned bite-size pieces delicately laid out on your plate. This is Crudo style, and the Crudo sampler is the way it should be done – with a different culinary adventure in every bite. Walk underneath the giant front window and you'll hit a room of brass table tops glowing with oil lamp lighting. Fiddly little dishes are scattered uniformly on every table next to delicate glassware filled with crisp aromatic whites. Alongside your Crudo sampler, get yourself a selection of freshly shucked oysters, some of which have been hauled straight out of places as close as Tomales Bay (see p. 142). Conversely, get your hands working a dungeness crab or half a Maine lobster and finish with a perfect cheese plate. Like any dependable San Francisco eatery, it's generally advisable to make a booking – but keep in mind that happy hour from 5–6.30pm is first in, best dressed.

POCKET TIP
When you've eaten, see if there's anything playing at The Independent across the street – often featuring local favourites, indie and up-and-coming acts.

10 SMUGGLER'S COVE

650 Gough St
415 869 1900
www.smugglerscovesf.com
Open Mon–Sun 5pm–1.15am
[MAP p. 178 A3, 181 E1]

Look for the glowing red light and bouncer, otherwise you won't be able to spot the entrance to an experience that should not be missed. This three-story tiki bar with tropical vibes is inspired by the legendary tiki bars of San Francisco past. I'd describe it as a pirate's bungalow spruced up by an imaginative Tahitian decorator – a glowing rockpool, drinks rested on rum crates and Caribbean motifs. You'll find what's rumoured as the most comprehensive rum stash in the US – 600 strong sitting on the shelf, several of which have been developed for Smuggler's Cove. The cocktail menu encompasses both the history of the rum cocktail, exotic cocktails from legendary tiki bars around the world and a selection of great house inventions. You'll find classics like planters punch and sidewinders fang, but the bartender will likely recommend their pride and joy – the rum barrel – a treasured secret recipe. They have a series of drinks that are designed to be shared, including some volcano-like boozy science experiments.

57

11 TORONADO

547 Haight St
415 863 2276
www.toronado.com
Open Mon–Sun 11.30am–2am
[MAP p. 180 C4]

This part of San Francisco is littered with dive bars; through swinging saloon doors, you'll hit outdated jukeboxes and faded beer memorabilia, so why would I send you in the direction of one in particular? Beer. Few other bars on the strip or even perhaps in the entire city have such broad-ranging beer options. Not to mention, knowledge of the brews' background and a genuine appreciation for the amber fluid. The taps change daily, there's a large list rotating on the bulkhead in the middle of the main room. The beers are categorised by brewery and not style; if it's all a bit confusing the staff will take great pleasure in helping you out. A large neon sign above the bar reads 'garage service', heavy metal screeches in the background and the sound of pint glasses clinking can be heard from every direction. There's no food and it's cash only, but there's an ATM in the back and plenty of food to be found on the same street. You'll find some good looking merch in the back room if you've enjoyed the place so much that you need a memento.

NOB HILL, CHINATOWN & POLK STREET

Nob Hill is an elevated point of the Golden City and is pretty much up and down, so you'll get a good workout. But you'll also feel like a local with corner stores, Mom and Pop joints, residential folk walking dogs and punters sitting in their local after work watching a game. Sitting on a higher plane at the top of a steep Nob Hill walk is Grace Cathedral (see p. 64), an incredibly peaceful part of the city.

Nestled between Nob Hill and the Financial District (FIDI), Chinatown has been thriving since the gold rush days, and Chinese immigrants' cultural contributions have been integral to the city's development. You'll know when you get there from the hanging lanterns and immediate change in building motifs and signage. You can even preserve your fortune inside a cookie at the Golden Gate Fortune Cookie Factory (see p. 62).

A street away from Van Ness, the arterial road, perpendicularly sits Polk Street. Polk is the home of some of my favourite San Francisco locations – the ones that frequently pop up as recommendations from people I trust, names like Swan Oyster Depot (see p. 69), Bob's Donuts and Pastries (see p. 72 and Tommy's Joynt (see p. 65). The kind of places unique to this city, filled with the kind of character that gives the city character, too.

This hilly part of the city is fantastic for photography, so be sure to bring your camera and tripod. My favourite spot is the streets surrounding Huntington Park – there's a different city panoramic in every direction.

Train (BART): Montgomery St.

→ View of the Transamerica Pyramid from Nob Hill's hilly streets

JONES
300

1 GOLDEN GATE FORTUNE COOKIE FACTORY

56 Ross Alley
415 806 8243
www.goldengatefortunecookies.
com
Open Mon–Fri 9am–6.30pm,
Sat–Sun 9am–7pm
[MAP p. 174 B3]

Generally regarded as a must-see location – the Fortune Cookie Factory is hidden at the end of an unsuspecting alley. You'll have to walk through in single form to witness the magic that is fortune-cookie creation. The walls are lined with bags and bags of cookies, coming in multiple shapes and sizes, some coated in chocolate, some covered with sprinkles and some the size of footballs. One of the more unique experiences is the chance to craft your own fortune and have it secured in crispy sweet biscuit ready to be handed onto a mate as a practical joke or a loving sentiment. The choice is yours. Don't take photos unless you're willing to pay for them, and be prepared to buy something.

REGULAR
ADULT X RATED
35 PCS BAG
$6.00

2 CABLE CAR MUSEUM

1201 Mason St
415 474 1887
www.cablecarmuseum.org
Open Mon–Sun 10am–5pm
Nov–Mar, 10am–6pm Apr–Oct
[MAP p. 174 A3]

The sound of cable cars rattling in the background is about as San Francisco as fog, Giants' caps and the faint smell of weed. Here's your chance to really get to the bottom of how cable cars work and what lies beneath this city. Spoiler alert: it's 17,200 metres (56,430 feet) of cabling. The system was actually designed to replace the omnibus (horse-drawn system), however, was ill-equipped to face the tumultuous hills of San Francisco. From the viewing deck, you can see the remaining four of the original 23 cables in operation – cables being looped for all four cable car routes: City Mason, Hyde, California and Powell. You'll also have the chance to learn a bit more about the routes of yesteryear and understand precisely how widespread the reach of the system used to be. You'll see scale models of the original replica cars and footage of the devastation of the 1906 earthquake, too.

POCKET TIP

For a quick stop-off at a novel location, pop into the Gallery Cafe across the street – it's eclectically decorated, filled with games and plays vintage horror films certain nights of the week.

3 GRACE CATHEDRAL

1100 California St
www.gracecathedral.org
[MAP p. 183 F2]

Grace Cathedral has existed since the gold rush days but, like most of San Francisco, got floored by the earthquake in 1906 and was rebuilt bigger and better. The present structure began construction in 1964. Designed in French Gothic style, it's now the third largest episcopal cathedral in the nation. Mark Twain wrote about it in a newspaper, Martin Luther King Junior preached a sermon in it and many people come to San Francisco to visit it annually. It's always been centered on aiding in social justice – it reached out in support during the AIDS crisis and in periods of racial injustice in the '60s – and it's considered a place of immunity today. The labyrinth in the middle is designed to be walked at a slow pace, so calm your mind and open your thoughts as you view the stunning murals and paintings. There's a suggested donation, tours at a price (book online), worship on Wednesday nights, a service on Sunday morning and a choir singing each evening. Printed guides are in multiple languages and events are listed on its website.

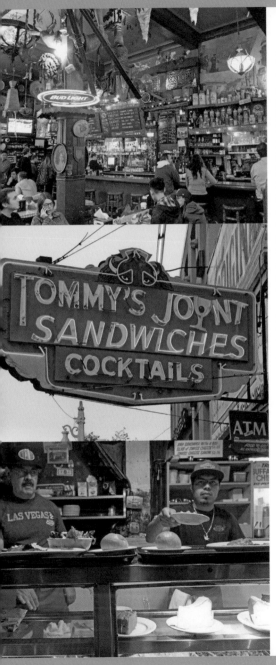

4 TOMMY'S JOYNT

1101 Geary Blvd
415 775 4216
www.tommysjoynt.com
Open Mon–Sun 10am–1.30am
[MAP p. 178 B1, 183 D4]

Hanging above the entrance
the sign reads: 'Welcome
Stranger', a sentiment that
remains throughout the
entire experience at Tommy's
Joynt – the Golden City's most
uniquely decorated dive bar
meets super-sized Sunday
carvery. It dishes up the most
generous portions of food I've
seen, at what can only be
tagged as recession prices
(and since Tommy's endured a
few recessions, it knows how
to do it right). Enjoy brisket,
turkey, pastrami and more in
the form of 'Tommy's Great Big
Sandwiches' for $8.75, and the
'Daily Dinner' plates for $12.90.
As you graze, you'll discover
an interior rivalled in comfort
only by the taste of the food.
You'll be seated amongst Bay
Area artefacts and anything
from a four-foot plastic bass to
a Bavarian cuckoo clock. With
bottles of beer as low as $2.75
and pints as low as $4, there's
no rush to leave. Tommy's is
old-school and naturally cash-
only. There might be a queue,
but these guys are carvery
veterans, and as they say: 'it
moves faster than the time it
takes to walk to the next place'.

5 THE GRUB/TAKE

1525 Pine St
415 673 8268
sfgrubstake.com
Open Mon–Fri 5pm–4am, Sat–
Sun 9am–4am
[MAP p. 183 D3]

Ever wondered what it would
be like if a cable car served
top-notch northern Californian
diner fare? Maybe not. But
if so, you need wonder no
further. Grubstake, well at
least half of it, is a converted
trolley – with red vinyl booth
seating and whimsical
handpainted Victorian-style
walls. Unlike the cable cars of
yesteryear, the Grub operates
on weekends from 9am to
4am (yes, not pm), serving
the Nob Hill residents both
the last meal of the day and
the first meal of the morning
with a smile. French dips, club
sandwiches and affordable cuts
of steak have been popping out
of the kitchen since 1976. The
menu also offers a Portuguese
Scrampled Eggs, based on the
chef's hometown cuisine. If
you're hitting the cafe early, I'd
recommend Joe's special – a
local favourite scrambled egg
dish that was first served at
Original Joe's.

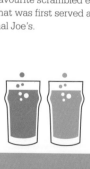

6 GOOD MONG KOK

1039 Stockton St
415 397 2688
Open Sat–Tues 7am–6pm
[MAP p. 174 B3]

You'd be excused for wandering past this place without noticing it. Firstly because of the queue obscuring the entire shopfront, secondly because of the incredibly worn signage, and thirdly because it's set in the middle of a row of shops that visibly seem quite similar. But they aren't …Good Mong Kok specialises in what can only be described as authentic and affordable for any budget. For just a few dollars each, you can have baked or steamed treats on the run or take them home. The non-stop cooking makes freshness the absolute key. Every order is basically pulled straight out of the steamer to order – dim sum, pork buns, bean buns, shrimp dumplings. All are available baked or steamed. Or you might choose the turnip cakes and sticky rice. My advice is to arrive half an hour before lunch to avoid the ever-present queues. Keep in mind this place is closed for like half the week!

7 SWAN OYSTER DEPOT

1517 Polk St
415 673 1101
Open Mon–Sat 10.30am–
5.30pm
[MAP p. 183 D2]

You can't really miss the bright blue canopy hovering over the corner of California and Polk streets, or the queue running 50 metres down the street. As the adage goes: 'good things come to those who wait'. In this circumstance, the good thing is a cup of piping hot creamy chowder, a bowl of freshly pulled crab louis or a dozen oysters hauled straight out of the Pacific. Seating is restricted to a single row of counter seating. It's snug and cosy, so I wouldn't want you to walk in with a rucksack. The guy in the white apron that takes your order is the same guy that's going to shovel shrimp onto your plate. You can spend as little or as much as you want – crab backs are $8 and a mixed dozen oysters are $32. The seafood salad is a great way of doing it on the cheap. Delving into crudo plates and sea urchin can quickly rack you up a $100 tab, though, so be sure to keep count because it's a cash-only establishment with no ATM.

8 MAC'D

2127 Polk St
www.getmacd.com
415 673 1101
Open Mon–Thurs & Sun 11am–
9pm, Fri–Sat 11am–2am
[MAP p. 183 D1]

Through the cheesy orange doorway under a neon sign, you'll head to the counter and have the 'build your own mac and cheese experience' that you've always wished for. I'm just going to rattle off a few of the choices here: bacon, corn, broccoli, cauliflower, chicken, crab, shrimp, tomato, peas, chorizo, jalapeño, pesto. And yes, the server tells me there have undoubtedly been occasions where people come in and ask for absolutely everything on that list. Although this seems like perhaps an impossible feat, they actually have gluten-free and lactose-free options. Cauliflower has never tasted so good.

POCKET TIP
There's a Russian Hill (1517 Polk St) location of MAC'D so no matter which side of town you're on, you can always get that cheesy fix.

9 TONGA ROOM & HURRICANE BAR

950 Mason St
www.tongaroom.com
415 772 5278
Open Wed–Thurs & Sun
5–11pm, Fri–Sat 5pm–12am
[MAP p. 174 A4]

Once you get past the awkwardness of walking through the lobby of one of the most expensive hotels in San Francisco, you'll encounter one of the great tiki bars of the world. Shareable punch bowls, Tahitian cane chairs, straw huts, the mast of a ship marooned in 1947 and a pool, once swum in by bohemians that's now an artificial monsoon pond (it actually 'rains' every 30 minutes). The bar serves up all of the classic tiki drinks: mai thai, planters punch and the aptly named overproof zombie. The menu's Hawaiian, Mexican and Chinese, if that makes any sense. Prices are reasonable and you can enjoy Kahlua pork tacos, kimchi miso soup and ahi tuna poke tacos. Or get the Tonga pupu platter and share it with a large bowl of planters punch and some friends. There's some great photos and old menus in the foyer if you enjoy a glimpse of bygone days. The venue fills up fast, but there's always standing room for a cocktail or two.

10 BOB'S DONUTS
AND PASTRIES

1621 Polk St
www.bobsdonutssf.com
415 776 3141
Open Mon–Sun 24 hours
[MAP p. 183 D2]

The people's donut; that sweet friend you can call on any time of day. This is one of those Mom and Pop joints that makes a city – it's been there since the '50s and had the same owner since the '70s. Over 300 donuts are freshly baked each day, tried and true old-fashioned donuts – both raised and buttermilk. But when choosing, it's always best to decide on what's hot. The crew are continually experimenting, bringing flavours you might never expect, such as miso and sesame. See the big pink boxes sitting on the bar bench? If you can get a donut down that touches all four corners of this box in under two minutes, you're officially titled one of Bob's superstars. Your achievement will be forever marked on Bob's wall next to the table you sat at. I should highlight that the experience at 4am on a Saturday is an entirely different experience to during the day. After the bars close, the wolves come out and they want their freshly glazed dough – and fast!

PRE/IDIO, OUTER /UN/ET & LAND/ END

For a different side of the city in terms of geography, scene and setting, the laidback vibe in Sunset is quite a contrast to the high-rise bustling image you might have of metropolitan San Francisco. It's like the California dream Brian Wilson from the Beach Boys had in mind – relaxing, chilled and a place to smell the salty air, while watching folks meander past in flip-flops carrying paper parcels of fish and chips from Hook Fish Co, (see p. 88), and freshly baked bread from Outerlands (see p. 84). Strolling Balboa and Noriega streets, you'll pass sun-bleached trucks with surfboards stacked on top. Perhaps an old man strumming the ukulele and a friendly off-leash collie. The rightly named precinct is home to a sunset over the ocean that's well worth the wait.

Just north of the most western point of Golden Gate Park sits Lands End (see p. 80). Literally at the land's end, you'll find incredible coastal views and hiking trails filled with cypress trees and meandering rocky paths.

Sprawling further around the coast towards South Bay, you'll encounter Presidio, eventually culminating at the Marina District. Presidio, a semi-military owned region, is pristine in the truest sense of the word. There's perfectly manicured lawns, uniform red-brick houses, public gardens and coastal viewpoints fitted with convenient seating and kick-ass views, intertwined with family friendly places like The Walt Disney Family Museum (see p. 76) and The Wave Organ (see p. 77).

Light rail (Muni metro): Judah & 19th Ave for Outer Sunset

Bus: 48th Ave & Point Lobos Ave stop for Presidio and Lands End

→ Baker Beach and view of the Golden Gate Bridge

SIGHTS
1. The Walt Disney Family Museum
2. The Wave Organ
3. Palace of Fine Arts
4. Lands End

SHOPPING
5. Mollusk Surf Shop
6. General Store

EATING
7. Outerlands
8. Louis' Restaurant
9. Hook Fish Co

1 THE WALT DISNEY FAMILY MUSEUM

104 Montgomery St
415 345 6800
www.waltdisney.org
Open Mon & Wed–Sun
10am–6pm
[MAP p. 192 C3]

Walt Disney was nominated for 59 Academy Awards and personally won 32. His legacy lives on in many movies but this museum is an engaging and insightful look behind-the-scenes at the mastermind – Disney's risk, process, struggle, success and magic. The museum is set on large green lawns, in a row of pristine red-brick houses with a great view of the Golden Gate Bridge. You'll enter the museum to a full fanfare of Disney music. There are 17 rooms to see, full of immersive and fun activities, from creating your own cartoon soundtrack to a scaled-down replica of the original Disneyland vision (a crazy model of the town). You can sit at the desk Mickey was first drawn at to gain an appreciation for the techniques, processes and camerawork. There's also a series of workshops and community engagement programs throughout the year aimed at inspiring young artists. There's two films screened per day, which are only an extra $5 added onto your ticket.

POCKET TIP
If you're at the museum on a Sunday, start or finish at the Presidio Picnic – a fantastic local food truck initiative.

2 THE WAVE ORGAN

83 Marina Green Dr
www.exploratorium.edu/visit/
wave-organ
Open Mon–Sun 24 hours
[MAP p. 193 F1]

For me, this unique art-meets-nature project is purely what San Francisco is all about. Walk along the marina and you'll discover a sculpture almost camouflaged between the jetty and the sea. Created in 1986, this Exploratorium-funded project (*see* p. 3), by Peter Richards and George Gonzalez, is made from marble and granite. Some of the marble and granite was recycled from a cemetery up in Laurel Heights and stone from the city's kerbsides was also used. It's a place where you can listen to wave acoustics as tidal movements are recycled into a piece of art. You listen to the tones produced by the waves below via a submerged allotment of underground organ pipes – a harmony of the natural environment. The sound is at its best during high tide and also during a full moon. Alongside the sounds, you can contemplate the views across San Francisco Bay – on a clear day you'll see the Golden Gate Bridge, Alcatraz (*see* p. 6) and even Angel Island.

77

3 PALACE OF FINE ARTS

3601 Lyon St, Marina District
415 563 6504
www.palaceoffinearts.org
Open Mon–Sun 24 hours
[MAP p. 193 D3]

This massive theatre and exhibition space can be seen from anywhere within the Marina District. Generally, visitors will go and sprawl on the relaxing lawns surrounding it. It's well worth the visit just to see the fountains spouting around the stunning Graeco-Roman rotunda lying in the middle of a massive artificial lagoon. You can visit by day and enjoy views of the stunning exhibition centre, photograph a few swans and take a fantastic selfie or two. By night, the structure is completely lit up and throwing reflections of fire orange against the lake and the foggy skyline. It's often hired out for corporate events, lavish weddings, television filming and fancy galas, but the theatre also hosts everything from punk rock festivals to stand-up comedy (check the website).

POCKET TIP
Close by is the marina for a great view of the Golden Gate Bridge and some downtime on the grassy areas. Check out the awesome Dynamo Donut and Coffee shop, too!

4 LANDS END

680 Point Lobos Ave
Open Thurs–Tues 9am–5pm,
Wed 9.30am–5pm
[MAP p. 170 A2]

Lands End is the perfect lookout for the dramatic coastline and a great place to walk. It's a short trip from the heart of San Francisco, with many public transport options, however, an Uber ride from downtown outside of peak hour traffic can be a good option. Visit **Sutro Baths**, once saltwater public pools that had a magnificent outlook over the coast; the views remain, but now you'll only see remains of the baths. Walking the grounds at sunset is a fantastic experience. The woodland area north-east of the baths is the starting point to a series of hiking trails that zigzag through dramatic cliff faces, woodland plains and cypress tree forests. The walk is moderate, and it takes around an hour to reach the end (towards San Francisco). A popular detour is to the **Lands End Viewpoint** – on a clear day you'll have a complete view of the Golden Gate Bridge. The walk culminates in the upmarket residential area of **Sea Cliff** and from here it's a short stroll down to one of the inner-city's most accessible beaches, **Baker Beach**. It offers a unique view of the **Golden Gate Bridge**.

POCKET TIP
The Cliff House is a historic restaurant located directly above Sutro Baths, and Louis' Restaurant (see p. 86) is a more affordable diner-style option.

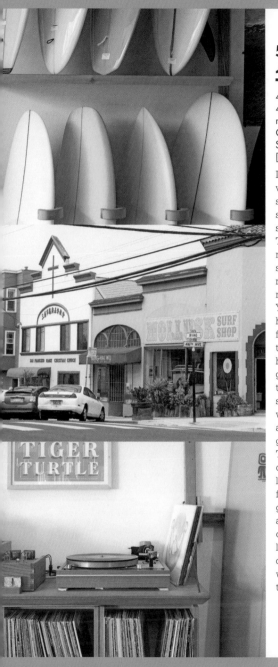

5 MOLLUSK SURF SHOP

4500 Irving St
415 564 6300
mollusksurfshop.com
Open Mon–Sat 10am–6.30pm,
Sun 10am–6pm
[MAP p. 191 B2]

In case you haven't felt the vibe yet, Sunset is a bit of a surfer's town, and every good seaside town needs a good surf shop (this one has a few). The folks at Mollusk shape, make and distribute their own surfboards and retail a killer range of their own threads, made right here in California. You'll find comfortable organic hemp-blend T-shirts and a few pieces in acid wash and tie-dye. It's all lightweight, hand-stitched and lookin' good. If you're actually on that California surf trip, they stock used boards, wetsuits, wax, local surf guides and anything else you'll need to get yourself out in the water. The fit-out is pretty next level, constructed with the aid of local carpenters (wood wizards) from Woodshop. A cool little art gallery is wedged to one side, and there's a feature room up a circular staircase (literally next level). The staff are very cool dudes that all know the area well if you're looking for where to find the best break.

6 GENERAL STORE

4035 Judah St
415 682 0600
www.shop-generalstore.com
Open Mon–Sun 11am–7pm
[MAP p. 191 B3]

This is one of those little gems you walk into without quite knowing what they sell – a beautifully curated space, like that Pinterest wall you've put together titled 'someday house'. It boasts a far-out collection of knick-knacks and gifts, such as racks of overalls and clogs, upcycled vintage, handcrafted jewellery of silver and gold, lip balm, oils, candles and a catalogue of interesting book titles by Georgia O'Keeffe and Ruth Asawa, and old Donald Judd Essays. Many of the wares are locally made and one of a kind. If you're new to the neighbourhood and looking to decorate your house, there's also room decor – from geometric stone hanging pieces to macramé. It's pretty hard to walk out of here without an Outer Sunset souvenir popping out the top of your backpack. If you walk through the rear door, there's a super cute little garden with old penny boards hanging off the fence.

POCKET TIP
Just next door is the illustrious Trouble Coffee, with the owner's story of community that results exclusively in the sale of coffee, buttered toast, coconuts and grapefruit juice.

GENERAL
STORE

FUCK IT,
I LOVE
YOU.

7 OUTERLAND/

4001 Judah St
415 661 6140
www.outerlandssf.com
Open Mon–Sun 9am–3pm,
5–10pm
[MAP p. 191 B3]

This humble, cosy breakfast
cafe evolves by dinnertime
into a more sophisticated bar/
restaurant with a party vibe.
It's the brainchild of a down-
to-earth surfer/carpenter/
baker team who have a habit
of collecting wood. The owner
tells me there's something
about fog rolling in over the
beach on a cold morning
that really matches freshly
baked bread, and I couldn't
agree more – and neither can
the locals, who consider it
a staple. There is one bread
dish that stands out to me
above the others, and that is
the incredible oozy cast-iron
grilled cheese sandwich.
Of course, there are fresh
salads and delicious pastries,
too. Carpenters from local
Woodshop have fitted out
the cafe, and every surface
and even the light fittings
look custom-built. The bowls
and crockery are made by
local Heath Ceramics, which
adds a very visual pleasure –
as if what's being plated
isn't enough!

8 LOUIS' RESTAURANT

902 Point Lobos Ave
415 387 6330
louissf.com
Open Mon–Sun 6.30am–6pm
[MAP p. 170 A3]

Talk about a table with a view,
a view that in fact has been
sought-after for years – this
cliff-face restaurant has been
owned since 1937 by the same
family. From your leather booth,
you would have used to have
seen the **Sutro Baths** (*see*
p. 80), but now it's the rugged
and sweeping bay. I had the
honour of being served by
the original owner's (Louis)
granddaughter, who tells me
that patrons keep coming
back – this is confirmed by a
man turning around to tell me
he's been getting the curly
fries and chocolate milkshake
for 30 years. Louis' has a pretty
amazing dedication to locally
sourced goods – they use eggs
produced within 160 kilometres
(100 miles) and everything else
that's put on a plate comes
from within 320 kilometres
(200 miles). Even the tiles you
stand on are made from 50 per
cent recycled content, and the
grease your chips are fried in is
locally turned into biofuel.

9 HOOK FIƧH CO

4542 Irving St
www.hookfishco.com
Open Mon–Thurs 8–11am
& 11.30am–9pm, Sat–Sun
9am–9pm
[MAP p. 191 B2]

Like moths to a flame, people
head to the beach for fish and
chips on a sunny day. But
surfer brothers, Chris and Bo,
pondered the concept on a
bike riding/fishing trip through
Baja and came up with a
completely different idea. With
the continual support of the
local fishing community, these
guys focus on traceability and
environmental consciousness
that reduces the food miles it
takes to get their product into
your hand. And the results are
in – the best fish and chips
you'll ever taste, served with
a cold bottle of beer. If you're
wondering which fish to get
fried up – of course, freshest is
best – the black cod and king
salmon are up there on my
recommended list. The other
dishes have a bit of a Mexican
twist, such as ceviche, tacos
and guacuamole. You can also
grab yourself crab and oysters
at a far more affordable price
than you'll regularly find in the
Bay Area. Fish for breakfast?
YES, please! From 8–11am,
albacore and tuna chorizo in a
great breakfast sandwich and
burritos are served through the
breakfast window!

POCKET TIP
3 Fish Studios is just across the street with stellar artwork from local makers.

/OUTH BEACH, /OMA & CIVIC CENTER

You can see the South Beach neighborhood starting to form as you head beyond the southern side of the Ferry Building (see p. 2) under the Bay Bridge. You'll see bayside food joints and a few bars charging for the ocean view, so finding the affordable gems requires a bit of research. Before heading south though, you'll hit the famous Oracle Park (see p. 93), home of the city's baseball team and pride: the hard-hitting Giants.

Inland towards the centre is SOMA (South of Market Avenue). Along Powell and Market streets, you'll come across global retail giants and department stores on the lower levels of the city's prominent high-rises. A stone's throw north, a collection of opulent hotels and upmarket retailers line Union Square (see p. 192) and the surrounding avenues. Throughout these streets, too, are a list of San Francisco's famous clubs, lounges and restaurants – the kind your grandparents went to as kids but still like to visit for nostalgia.

Civic Center (see p. 95) falls west of here and is the more monumental side of San Francisco, with grand Roman architecture and institutions like City Hall and stalwart art spaces like the Asian Art Museum.

On the outer edge of Civic Center lies Tenderloin (the Loin), a soulful and culturally rich neighbourhood. However, at times is has a less-than-desirable reputation, so it's important to have a plan and a direction and perhaps an Uber driver.

Train (BART): Civic Center, Powell St.

→ Artists in Union Square

1 UNION /QUARE

[MAP p. 176 C2]

Union Square is a vast
public plaza, enclosed by
Geary, Powell, Post and
Stockton streets. It makes for
a pleasant stroll through the
gardens and palm trees, and
there are often folks busking,
selling artworks or just soaking
up some sun. At the centre
stands the 26-metre-tall
(85 feet) **Dewey Monument**,
commemorating the Battle
of Manila Bay during the
Spanish–American War. It's
overlooked by a considerable
number of high-end hotel
chains and **Tiffany & Co**,
Macy's, **Apple Store**,
Bloomingdale's, **Nordstrom**,
Saks and other big-brand
stores. Just around the corner
to the east on Post and Geary
streets, you'll find just about
every luxury fashion brand
your average person can't
afford. As this is an upmarket
tourist area, food and booze
can be a little posh, but a short
walk away you'll find some
excellent diners like **Sears
Fine Food** (439 Powell St),
for great Swedish pancakes
and **Lori's** (500 Sutter St) for
traditional diner fare. Union
Square is reasonably accessible
by various public transport
options and just down the
street from several BART
(train) stations.

POCKET TIP

From Union Square, The
Theater District (Geary,
Sutter streets) is just a
short walk away, with a
range of great theatres
performing Broadway
musicals daily.

2 ORACLE PARK

24 Willie Mays Plaza
www.mlb.com/giants
[MAP p. 190 B4]

Originating in New York and
eventually migrating to San
Francisco in 1958, the Giants
have become the beating
heart of San Francisco for
sports fans. Since 2000, Oracle
Park has been the team's
home. The park is considered
one of the most picturesque
sporting venues in the world,
due to its views of the bay.
Baseball season runs from
approximately April until
October. Even if you don't
follow it, the experience of
watching a ball game, with a
hot dog, some garlic fries and
cold Anchor beer is fantastic.
Speaking of food, before the
game head to the **Public
House** opposite the park for
some greasy food and a cold
beer – it's a rite of passage.
Also, before a game, go to the
dug-out (the fan shop) to get
your baseball cap (you'll need
it to fit in). Remember to bring
your coat year-round as a foggy
cold front is always rolling into
the stadium from over the bay.
Tickets can cost anywhere
from $10 to $200, depending
on where you sit, the day of the
week and who is playing.

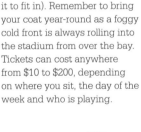

93

3 SALESFORCE PARK

425 Mission St
Open Mon–Sun 6am–9pm
[MAP p. 175 E4, 177 E1]

San Francisco's answer to
The New York City Highline,
this 5.4 acre inner city park
is filled with 17,000 plants,
helping provide carbon
dioxide and ventilation to
the modernised **Salesforce
Transit Center**. The center
is an active transit hub that
lays at the base of the tallest
skyscraper in San Francisco's
skyline, the **Salesforce Tower**
(previously Transbay). The
park filters stormwater, is a
beaconing habitat for local
wildlife and a unique spot to go
for a downtown stroll amongst
plants from California, such as
local redwoods (which I learned
from the park placards can
grow larger than the Statue of
Liberty!). It's a great spot to
have lunch and don't worry
if you haven't packed any, as
what's being labelled as **Food
Truck Alley** runs during lunch
hours and changes daily on the
ground level outside. You'll find
live music, board games to rent
and artists-in-residence with
their canvases out. This is one
San Francisco park I wouldn't
bring your dog or your cooler of
booze! Please.

4 CIVIC CENTER

sfciviccenter.org
[MAP p. 178 C3]

All the major attractions of
Civic Center sit as independent
French Beaux Arts-style
grand buildings that surround
a central grassy square. To
the east is the **Asian Art
Museum**, showcasing the
diversity and strength of
creativity amongst Asian
cultures, both contemporary
and historical. Filled with a
myriad of amazing pieces, the
gallery aims to be 'respectful,
engaging, inspirational, agile
and accessible'. Here you'll
see ivory carvings that date
back 5000 years, intricate snuff
boxes from last century and
a replica Japanese tea house.
It's $25 entry, and there's a
lovely cafe on the ground floor
that serves a mixture of Asian
cuisines. Directly opposite on
the west side is **City Hall**,
with monumental interiors
and decorative grandeur.
You'll need to clear security,
but walking around costs
absolutely nothing. Head to
the elevator to the left of the
entry, up to the mezzanine
level for a great view of a 1915
masterpiece – a gold-leafed
dome. There's a one-hour tour
at 10am, 12pm and 2pm. The
much-loved **Bill Graham
Civic Auditorium** is also here
and has hosted hundreds of
world-renowned musicians.

POCKET TIP
Other Civic Center
landmarks include the War
Memorial, Opera House,
the SF Jazz Center and the
Public Library. On the lawns,
you'll often find pop-up
artworks and events.

5 SAN FRANCISCO MUSEUM OF MODERN ART (SFMOMA)

151 3rd St
415 357 4000
www.sfmoma.org
Open Mon–Tues 10am–5pm,
Thurs 10am–9pm, Fri–Sun
10am–5pm
[MAP p. 177 D2]

Arrive early and start on the upper levels in one of the largest modern art collections in the world, with 33,000 works of art across a range of different media. SFMOMA reopened in mid-2016 after a massive expansion. Here you can get amongst some of the world's greats, including Jackson Pollock, Frida Kahlo, Andy Warhol and Francis Bacon. I recommend the app with audio guides, interactive stories and monologues. There's a series of rotating exhibits on level four – I enjoyed a printer continuously pumping out news stories. I also got to see the famous delicately strong spiders by Lewitt, Louise Bourgeois. Visit the outdoor sculpture garden and the central atrium and take in some fantastic downtown views. Have one of San Francisco's best coffees at **Sightglass** – or refuel in **Cafe 5** or **In Situ**. Museum entrance is adults $25, age 19–24 (with ID) $19.

POCKET TIP
If you have a San Francisco CityPASS, bring it to SFMOMA as you might save up to 45 per cent off the entry fee.

6 RED'S JAVA HOUSE

Pier 30
415 777 5626
www.redsjavahouse.com
Open Mon–Fri 7am–6pm,
Sat–Sun 9am–6pm
[MAP p. 190 B2]

Nestled basically under the Bay Bridge, you'll find a stocky little storefront that's been feeding the hardworking longshoreman and dock workers of South Beach since 1955. Opened by a couple of (once) red-headed paperboys, Tom and Mike McGarvey, Red's has become a stalwart intergenerational favourite. Red's actually claims its only addition to the menu since its opening was french fries in the year 2000. Its simple menu is kept alive by the likes of the go-to burger made with sourdough bread, onions, pickles and yellow mustard – always without lettuce and tomato; always. This is under $6 and is perfect washed down with a cold pint of Lagunitas beer at a combined cost of $10. You'll find a few other burger options, hot dogs and fish and chips, too. Personally, I like to head in for the breakfast experience – it's a quieter time, and Red's serves up full plates of eggs, sausage and hashbrowns just the way I like them. You can sit inside amongst the South Beach relics or outside overlooking the ocean and the bridge.

7 THE BIRD

115 New Montgomery St
415 872 9825
www.thebirdsf.com
Open Mon–Wed 7.30am–9pm,
Thurs–Fri 7.30am–10pm, Sat
9am–8pm
[MAP p. 177 E2]

A friend working in SOMA recommended I check this place out for lunch one day, and I rocked up to find a line stretching around the block. It's worth the wait, but the place is small, so you may have to eat on the move. This isn't just any chicken sandwich; this is the 'ultimate fried chicken sandwich', sold for as low as $8. The free-range chicken is cooked with a special berbere spice blend and served on a bun that's freshly baked each morning and topped with housemade crunchy apple slaw. If you thought that sentence was a mouthful, just wait until you get the sandwich! To complement your chicken sandwich, choose a tin of beer (the selection is pretty decent) or make it a 'happier meal' for $12.50 and add some curly fries in there. If you're here early, there's a breakfast option, too – served on a biscuit bun and hashbrown on the side.

8 BELDEN PLACE

Belden Place, between Pine &
Bush streets
www.belden-place.com
[MAP p. 174 B4, 177 D1]

Belden Place, Belden Alley,
Belden Lane or Belden Street –
whatever you call it – is
known by many locals as the
French part of San Francisco.
In close proximity to the
Alliance Française, the French
Consulate and the Notre-Dame-
des-Victoires Church (where
you can still hear a service in
French), it's not hard to see
why. The stretch itself is an
alfresco or 'en plein air' dining
strip running between Pine
and Bush streets. On a warm
summer's night, the streets
are filled with patrons sitting
curbside in one of the many
eateries, under fairy lights,
swirling glasses of pinot and
nibbling on baguettes spread
with soft cheese and pâté. In
the breezy months, folks sit
cosily inside the provincially
decorated restaurants, under
candlelight amongst the
sounds of Edith Piaf and Joey
Dassin. You can window shop
for food but don't feel pressure
from the host spruiking you
out the front – take your time,
read the menus, ask for a
discounted bottle of wine and
follow your gut.

POCKET TIP
Although the location
has built itself a French
reputation, in more
recent years Italian and
Catalonian restaurants
have popped into
the mix too.

9 TEMPE/T

431 Natoma St
415 495 1863
Open Mon–Sun 12pm–2am
[MAP p. 176 C4, 179 F2]

Entering off a side street through what seems like an insignificant doorway, you'll find a bar that typifies San Francisco dive-bar culture. Every surface, including the cash machine and pool table, is coated in graffiti tags, key-etched confessions of true love and crusty vinyl stickers. Light bleeds in over pitch-black tables through the barred windows. Patrons sit on bar stools alternating sips between their shot and beer. This sets the rugged charm but the major drawcard is the affordable prices. Selling pints of beer as low as $2, it's cheaper than drinking at home. I recommend the combos board for shot and beer pairings like the 'Donkey Show' and the 'Industry Special' (highlife and fernet) to do it right. Food can be ordered from 'the box' outside – the menu reads: burgers, mac and cheese, fried chicken and garlic fries. The box opens at 4.20pm but some food is available inside 12pm to 3pm. The house rules of pool should be mentioned – hit a ball on the floor and pay a buck. Get the 8 ball in on the break and win the jackpot.

SOUTH BEACH, SOMA &
CIVIC CENTER

10 WHITECHAPEL

600 Polk St
415 292 5800
www.whitechapelsf.com
Open Mon–Wed 5pm–12am,
Thurs–Sat 5pm–2am
[MAP p. 178 B2]

Check onto the platform
of Whitechapel, a London-
inspired steampunk bar, based
on the fictitious fantasies of
founders Martin Kate and
Alex Smith. It's essentially
a gin lab set in what looks
like an abandoned Victorian-
era London underground
(train) station. Glowing green
coils represent the key gin
botanicals. With a 700-strong
bottle back bar, it's the most
extensive collection of gin in
North America. The cocktail
menu (125–130 items) 100 per
cent contains traces of gin,
too. With mersey tunes like
Simon and Garfunkel and the
Kinks playing in the distance,
enjoy sipping house gin and
tonics and a negroni that you
can adjust yourself with an
eye-dropper to taste. The food
menu offers Bangladeshi and
British pub fare, but you'll also
find fresh fish and chips to tie
in with the London vibe. This
is a sketchy block so keep
your wits about you on the
way home!

POCKET TIP
The famous multi-themed
detective agency bar Wilson
& Wilson (505 Jones St), is a
San Francisco must-see. You'll
need their password, so why
not do a cocktail crawl and
try to get a booking at both
there and Whitechapel!

POCKET TIP

Local food trucks can be found at Anchor Public Taps in the courtyard at night – but they won't be there during the day, so don't come hungry.

11 ANCHOR PUBLIC TAPS

495 De Haro St
415 863 8350
www.anchorbrewing.com/
publictaps
Open Mon–Wed 12pm–9pm,
Fri–Sat 12pm–10pm, Sun
12pm–8pm
[MAP p. 189 E2]

Born out of the goldfields of the late 1800s, for close to 100 years Anchor brewed a sole beer – the California Common or steam ale that originated out of necessity when larger stocks of yeasts from Europe couldn't be kept refrigerated in the warmer climates. Today Anchor brews a range of styles, none more popular than Anchor Steam, which is about as commonplace in San Francisco as fog. But don't let its commonality fool you – it's loved by both the enthusiast and the penny-saving beer drinker alike (and it's the official beer of the Giants). The brewery is open daily, but I'd recommend doing a tour (check the website). At **Anchor Brewing Public Taps** 20 metres down the road, you can taste the entire range, come paddle or pint, in a large outdoor and indoor tasting room. You might want to grab that Lyft (rideshare) if you're considering filling up that growler, as it's a steep walk down back to town!

SOUTH BEACH, SOMA &
CIVIC CENTER

12 CITY BEER /TORE

1148 Mission St
415 503 1033
www.citybeerstore.com
Open Mon–Sun 12pm–12am
[MAP p. 179 D3]

Owners Craig and Beth
envisaged offering a wine
bar–style experience, except
replacing the wine with beer.
The idea that you'd have
to drink an entire six-pack
or a full pint of something
to experience it was a little
baffling to them. The process
here is about mixing and
matching. This tasting
bar-cum-bottle shop's the
ideal joint to pop in for a few
cheeky tasters and grab a
can or two to take back to
your accommodation. It's
a draft lovers oasis – with
28 dedicated taps and a couple
of hand pumps, and a spirited
focus on local brewers and
Californian brewcraft. The
bottle shop really is something
else – 10 fridges dedicated
to predominantly American
brews, so you're sure to find
something you've never come
across before. I managed to
pick up a piña colada gose and
a green tea berliner weisse!
With a calendar filled with
dedicated sipping sessions
and food pop-ups, it pays to
check the schedule before you
head in.

13 MIKKELLER BAR

34 Mason St
415 984 0279
mikkellerbar.com/sf
Open Sun–Wed 12pm–12am,
Thurs–Sat 12pm–2am
[MAP p. 176 B3, 179 D1]

With passion, hops, grain and yeast on his side, a Danish maths and science teacher took the world by storm as a nomadic brewer and then set up camp in California. The brick-and-mortar brewery is based in San Diego, and bars and brew collaborators can be found around the globe. I'd recommend trying some of the San Diego beers, like the windy new england or the raspberry blush. Otherwise, you can choose from the 40 taps, 2 cask handles and an overwhelming bottle collection. The sausage platter is a pretty good option and other shareables include the charcuterie and farmhouse cheese, much of which comes from dairies around the bay. For those who don't want to share, the California ranger (hotdog), the reuben with salad and the mac and cheese will pair nicely with your frothy. On weekends, head downstairs to the **Sour Room**, inclusive of 50-plus specialty bottles. Look through the little window and you'll see the unique flux capacitor – a device for perfect keg control for every single beer on tap.

MISSION & CASTRO

Mission's one of the oldest parts of the city and an area yet to fully gentrify. It's where you can still see a collision of multiculturalism and subcultures that coexist, all within a few major streets. It's the sort of place where you can sip chai tea at a skate shop right before you see a huge mural being painted down the laneway across the street.

The expected cuisine within the Mission is Mexican burritos (see p. 124). But there's an attractive sequence of restaurants, ranging from elegant special occasion places to street-corner bakeries, such as Tartine (see p. 122), pumping out fresh loaves by the hour.

Bars and nightlife are much the same – you'll find yourself in some hidden back room ordering a drink so fancy that it could be hung on the wall at SFMOMA (see p. 96), and the next round you'll walk across the street to a pinball arcade and drink a $3 tin of beer.

You can buy anything in Mission (except property if your saving schedule looks like mine) – from a taxidermy moose head at Paxton Gate (see p. 116), to a first-edition hardcover at Dog Eared Books (see p. 114). Even Piña Colada flavoured soft-serve at Bi-Rite Creamery (see p. 119).

Nearby, Castro – has been a flourishing space for the LGBTIQA+ community for years. Home to councilman Harvey Milk and the legacy he and many others before and after him have left behind, there are many iconic venues (see p. 110).

Train (BART): 24th St. Mission, 16th St. Mission

Light rail (Muni metro): Castro

→ Clarion Alley Street murals

1 CLARION ALLEY MURAL PROJECT (CAMP)

Clarion Alley, between Mission and Valencia streets
clarionalleymuralproject.org
[MAP p. 187 E2]

Originally titled Cedar Lane, Clarion Alley was, prior to 1992 before the collective begun, a completely blank laneway. Seriously, you can find photos online. Nearly thirty years later, the efforts of the Clarion Alley Mural Project (CAMP), an artists-run collective, has seen the creation of over 700 murals that run the entire length of this strip. The alley now gets visited by over 200,000 people annually. In general, the artists are up-and-coming Bay Area locals looking to get their message across in a public space, although CAMP often engages with other community initiatives from both near and afar. For the best part, the murals and the organisation are about promoting social justice. Works are themed socially and politically, and are community-oriented and aim for 'goals of social inclusiveness and aesthetic variety' (to quote its mission). A full list of artists and photographs of works, past and present, is available on its website. But I suggest that you head down and see firsthand this inspiring and creative space.

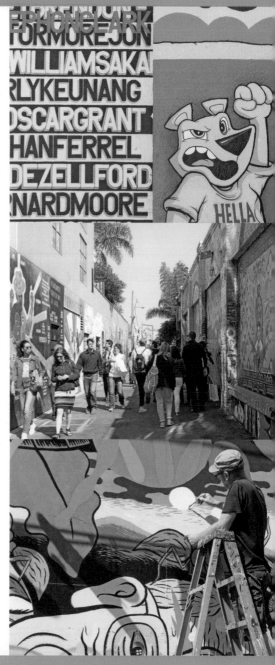

2 MISIÓN SAN FRANCISCO DE ASÍS (OLD MISSION DOLORES)

3321 16th St
415 621 8203
www.missiondolores.org
Open Sun–Fri 9.30am–4pm,
Sat 9am–4pm
[MAP p. 187 D2]

San Francisco is filled with a range of modern architectural marvels, but I think it's important to step back – a long way back to 1776 – to the time when the city was founded, when the formation of the oldest building in San Francisco commenced. Here you can experience two amazing chapels and a basilica designed in a Spanish style, coated with German stained glass and glittering with intricate motifs. All of this for a bargain $7. It's a peaceful escape; when I attended there wasn't another person in sight, and I could take my time strolling the mosaic floors and sitting amongst the dramatically high ceilings, getting as comfortable as possible on a hardwood pew. Lay a candle down in front of Guadalupe or visit the museum and learn the history of how the Spanish and the Native American people used to live in the area we now know as San Francisco.

3 LGBTIQA+ IN THE CASTRO

[MAP p. 181 D2]

There are several places of interest to get a glimpse of the rich history and culture of the LGBTIQA+ community here. A good place to start is the **GLBT Historical Society** (4127 18th St), a great museum with a collection of rotating exhibits that share the unique stories, pivotal characters and powerful movements that have shaped the city. You'll probably come across the **Rainbow Honor Walk** (Castro St), a collection of bronze plaques that detail the lives of LGBTIQA+ individuals who have contributed in pivotal ways to society. The walk is both inspiring and educational. You can visit **Harvey Milk's Old Camera Shop** (575 Castro St), the camera shop of Harvey Milk, which was the campaign headquarters for the famed openly gay American politician who held office from 1972–1978. The shop was once a key hub for the community. A nice end to the afternoon is at **Twin Peaks Tavern** (401 Castro St), often cited as the first gay bar in the nation, opened in 1935. This landmark location, also with the **Rainbow Flags**, is welcoming and the perfect spot to sit back and take in the neighbourhood.

4 UNIONMADE

493 Sanchez St
415 861 3373
www.unionmadegoods.com
Open Mon–Sat 11am–7pm,
Sun 12pm–6pm
[MAP p. 181 D2]

On the eastern edge of the
Castro precinct, you'll find
Unionmade, a store filled with
American-made menswear
with a touch of heritage and
nostalgia. Brands like Levis,
Carhartt and Pendleton are
thrown in with trophy finds
from Japan, Italy, France and
Scandinavia. Sharp cuts, bold
colours and creative patterns
line the racks. To the centre is
an on-point shoe shelf – boots,
loafers and sneakers with
brands like Alden, Redwing
and Clarks. The staff are
knowledgeable, patient and
above all else interested in
helping you craft a look that's
just right for you.

POCKET TIP
There's a Unionmade
womenswear store
(4035 18th St) just
up the street, crafted
similarly with labels
including Hartford.

UNIONMADE
WOMEN

5 EVERLANE

461 Valencia St
www.everlane.com
Open Mon–Sat 11am–8pm,
Sun 11am–7pm
[MAP p. 187 E1]

Everlane started as a group of local designers showcasing their wares as a collective. Everything here looks like it's right where it's supposed to be. It's a store full of clean-cut, chic, proper and affordable basics. Here you'll find simple box-cut T-shirts, leather sandals, silk shirts, cropped pants and chunky cotton sweaters. Everything is in natural colours of tan and navy blended with an array of washed-out tones of pastel and peach. The store is somewhat segmented into companion products, making it easy to piece together a completely new outfit. It's a bright space with entirely white surfaces and natural light. You'll see signs in-store for The Transparency Project – a set of direct links playing audio feeds to the locations where the clothing is being produced, from Los Angeles to Ho Chi Minh City in Vietnam.

6 DOG EARED BOOKS

900 Valencia St
415 282 1901
www.dogearedbooks.com
Open Mon–Sun 10am–10pm
[MAP p. 187 E3]

Every person living out of a backpack needs a paperback for the long bus trip or layover on their way to the next destination – so look no further. Here's a 20-year-old fantastic little bookstore in the heart of Mission. It's a general-interest bookstore that enthusiastically fills its shelves with a little bit of everything – old and new – and for decent prices, too. The space is the perfect collection of naturally lit shelves with handwritten signs and local artworks (for sale) hanging in every corner. For those interested in local literature, there's a selection of small press and locally published books and authors. There's also a great collection of travel books, field guides and maps for those new to San Francisco or looking to explore further. Should you venture to the Castro, there is a second store operating there, too (489 Castro St). Both stores stock an extensive range of LGBTIQA+ material. And the magazine selection is pretty comprehensive, too.

7 PAXTON GATE

824 Valencia St
415 824 1872
www.paxtongate.com
Open Sun–Wed 11am–7pm,
Thurs–Sat 11am–8am
[MAP p. 187 E3]

We are talking some real conversation starters when decorating your home, office or dungeon: T-rex teeth, a fossilised walrus penis and taxidermy giraffe, moose and just about every other animal – if it offends, avoid. There is, of course, a collection of things for the more vanilla collector too: a selection of intricate terrariums, indoor plants, crystals and a fascinating collection of books. Most items have come from private collectors, estate sales, research facilities and even museums themselves, so you never really know what it is that you're going to find. Classes are available on Saturdays and Sundays in the art of bug pinning, taxidermy and much more, which are accompanied by adult beverages.

POCKET TIP

Paxton Gate's Curiosities for Kids (766 Valencia St) is just down the street from Paxton Gate. The much-loved Pirate Supply Store (826 Valencia) for the young ones is just next door to Paxton Gate!

8 THERAPY STORES

545 Valencia St
415 865 0981
www.therapystores.com
Open Mon–Thurs 12pm–9pm,
Fri 12pm–10pm, Sat 11am–
10pm, Sun 11am–9pm
[MAP p. 187 E2]

Therapy is that reliable shop for when you have no idea what you're shopping for. A retail store perhaps as diverse as the foggy city itself. Wander in at the end of your trip and find gifts by local makers that suit your grandmother, six-year-old niece and philosophical flatmate. Since, like many stores in the area, it's open late, it really can be last minute. It's stocked with so much San Francisco and Californian stuff, such as curious combinations of patches, pins, socks, books, tea towels, mugs and other suitcase-friendly sized gifts. Witty slogans, ironic phrases, jokes and meme-ish designs are all in the mix somewhere. Then there's the racks at the back with dresses, T-shirts and shirts designed by Bay Area designers. If packing is an issue, you'll discover they sell stellar backpacks too! If you live in the city and a suitcase isn't actually an issue, shop for the collection of handpainted signs, jazzy sofa cushions and other homewares.

117

9 BETABRAND

780 Valencia St
415 692 7433
www.betabrand.com
Open Mon–Fri 11am–7pm, Sat
11am–6pm, Sun 12pm–6pm
[MAP p. 187 E3]

Betabrand has taken the crowdfunding concept of supply and demand direct to consumer voting in the fashion industry. A revolutionary idea that could only really come out of the Bay Area – a place where creativity and technology shake hands daily. You won't only be walking into the storefront but the studio of the designers, marketers and all of the other inner workings of the brand. Let me explain … all products have passed the test of user approval from an online voting system where users provide an insight as to the colour, texture and style of what they like. Every product runs at a limited supply, so everything you'll be looking at – from Barefoot Vivo collaborations to the spacesuit smart material jackets – will all be once-in a-lifetime buys. There's a specific travel section filled with wearable tech, such as a wrinkle proof jacket or a shirt with a demagnetised passport pocket! Perhaps you have an idea of your own you'd like to submit to the team.

10 BI-RITE CREAMERY

3692 18th St
415 626 5600
www.biritemarket.com/
creamery
Open Mon–Sun 12pm–9pm
[MAP p. 187 D2]

A stone's throw from **Bi-rite Market** (the go-to for years for locals getting locally grown produce, fruit and vegetables and preserves) is Bi-Rite Creamery. The ice-creamery follows the same traditions as the market, so only organically harvested local ingredients are used when making the ice-cream that's served both by the cone and by the pint. My favourite flavour is salted caramel, but other options include orange cardamom, black sesame, rose, earl grey, and peanut butter swirl. Next door there's a soft-serve window that changes what's on offer daily.

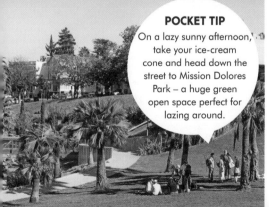

POCKET TIP
On a lazy sunny afternoon, take your ice-cream cone and head down the street to Mission Dolores Park – a huge green open space perfect for lazing around.

11 MISSION BOWLING CLUB

3176 17th St
415 863 2695
www.missionbowlingclub.com
Open Tues–Wed 3–11pm,
Thurs–Fri 3pm–12am, Sat
11am–12am, Sun 11am–11pm
[MAP p. 188 A2]

Run by three incredibly cool local ladies, not only is this an exceptionally cool retro set of polished bowling lanes, it's also a community space with a well-stocked bar filled with local booze (so local, in fact, that when I last visited, the beer on tap was being drunk by the brewer who was sitting at the bar). Then there's the bistro – serving all of the foods that go well with good friends and good times: think fried chicken, chilli fries and deviled eggs. All of the signage and sculptures on the front and rear were done by local artists, including the massive Mission Bowling Club sign. Rockabilly music rings out over the constant clattering of pins and balls speeding down polished wood, and it's really quite affordable – it's actually cheaper earlier on in the evening, so if you're flexible you can save some cash. And well, if you rock up and all of the lanes are taken, I doubt you have ever complained about having to sit down for a slick cocktail before.

12 TARTINE

600 Guerrero St
415 487 2600
www.tartinebakery.com
Open Mon 8am–7pm, Tues–
Wed 7.30am–7pm, Thurs–Fri
7.30am–8pm, Sat–Sun
8am–8pm
[MAP p. 187 E2]

Tartine is a name that's synonymous with 'flour power' in San Francisco. Folks have been known to endure several extra BART (train) stops just to get their hands on a fresh country loaf or a morning bun. There's street-side alfresco seating and some tables inside, too. It's hard to deny the freshness of the bread when you can literally watch it being kneaded and baked in front of you. My first Tartine experience was a vanilla bean custard tart lined with caramel, banana and hard chocolate, and I've had it each time I've been since. It's not all about the sweets though – there's a chalkboard of hot-pressed sandwiches, croissants, quiches and other savouries. If it's a Sunday morning and you need to clear your head, a passionfruit mimosa or a matcha latte would do the trick. A quick hint on the process – go up and order your pastries, then order your coffee, then walk around and pay at the register.

13 MIƧƧION CHINEƧE FOOD

2234 Mission St
415 863 5710
www.missionchinesefood.com
Open Mon–Wed 11.30am–3pm
& 5–10.30pm, Thurs–Sun
11.30am–3pm & 5–10.30pm
[MAP p. 187 F3]

This place is like a radical
Chinese New Year celebration,
with hanging lanterns, an
oversized dragon and a retro
ice-cold-drinks sign. DMX is
playing in the background,
as the floor staff try to contort
themselves through an over-
seated establishment. Your
plates literally chime with
those of the party sitting
next to you, but this isn't a
problem at all – you're all in
this together. Upon ordering,
I'd like to warn you the portion
sizes are fit for competition-
grade eaters. I'd highly suggest
the crazy rice and leave
the surprise to you. There's
probably going to be a line but
it moves fast, and if there is a
possible space to fit you, the
staff are up for the challenge.
After too many Tsingtao's,
the run for the bathroom is an
interesting experience, but I'll
leave that surprise to you as
well. Expect Uber Eats cyclists
running in and out, and keep
in mind that there is a daily
Chinese bento lunch special
for $15.

123

14 MI**SS**ION BURRITO

[MAP p. 187 E2]

There are hundreds of taquerias in the Bay Area, and in no other precinct are they as densely clustered as they are in Mission – hence the name Mission Burrito for the large tortilla filled with meat, beans, rice, salsa and queso served with a side of corn chips. **Taqueria La Cumbre** (515 Valencia St), **El Faro** (2399 Folsom St) and **Taqueria El Castillito** (136 Church St) are traditional little places filled with basic decor and mariachi music playing. A feed can come in under $10, including chips and a drink, and you can be in and out within 15 minutes. Most taquerias serve a range of Mexican beers: Corona, Modello and Tecate … some even Chiladas and it's not unknown to find dirt-cheap margaritas (as low as $5), too. There's also a string of more upmarket places if you're looking for formal table service. **Cadillac Bar and Grill** (Market Sq, 44 9th St) has always been a family favourite, and **Tacolicious** (741 Valencia St) offers a variety of Mexican flavours with a bar-style vibe. For vegan and ethically conscious diners, head to **Gracias Madre** (2211 Mission St).

125

15 HAWKER FARE

680 Valencia St
415 400 5699
www.hawkerfare.com
Open Mon–Fri 3–10pm, Fri–Sat
5.30–11pm, Sun 5.30–10pm
[MAP p. 187 E2]

Somewhat reminiscent of a bustling South-east Asian hawker centre, this one-stop shop puts out a variety of high-quality Isan and Lao dishes with an innovative take. Dine in a large and vibrantly decorated space filled with brightly coloured mismatched tablecloths and hanging lights. The food comes in moderate portion sizes and is all super decent quality. Four of us dined together, and the red curry noodles and spare ribs were a hit amongst everyone – and the rice ball salad, panang curry and green beans were pretty good, too. If you like a party, you will feel right at home as it's perfect for heading out with a group of friends for a night of fruity cocktails and spicy food amongst popping tunes. Be prepared to drink tiki-style tropical cocktails out of novelty ceramic mugs – perhaps a parrot, maybe an Easter Island head. You can head upstairs to the dedicated cocktail bar before or after and grab yourself another tiki delight. You deserve it.

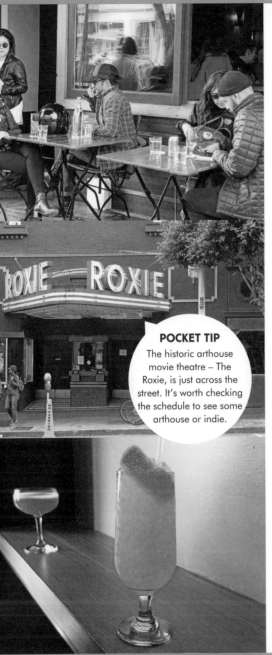

POCKET TIP

The historic arthouse movie theatre – The Roxie, is just across the street. It's worth checking the schedule to see some arthouse or indie.

16 ABV

3174 16th St
415 400 4748
www.abvsf.com
Open Mon–Sun 2pm–2am
[MAP p. 187 E1]

As you approach a row of motorcycles pulled up out the front, you can hear the overflow of upbeat music, mumbled conversations and ice clattering against steel. Listen carefully, for these are all signs of the type of bar you're about to walk into. ABV is one of the great cocktail bars of the district – a fantastic list of booze-forward tinctures organised by base spirit. If you're unsure, the golden rule in a joint like this is to ask the bartender – they'll surely help you find what you're hankering after. There's also a surprisingly good mocktail menu. What goes well with great cocktails is dirty snacks – and there's a fully-fledged bar menu you can nibble at, such as tater tots and sliders. I went with the 'spicy ass burger and chips', and it was in fact quite spicy. **Overproof**, the rotating, themed restaurant upstairs, is – from what I've heard – really worth a visit if you can get a booking.

127

17 THE BEEHIVE

842 Valencia St
415 282 8283
www.thebeehivesf.com
Open Mon–Thurs 5pm–12am,
Fri–Sat 2pm–2am, Sun 2pm–
12am
[MAP p. 187 E3]

This is one of the more recent bars added to Mission's small army of fine establishments. Upon entering, you'll instantly be greeted by a large marble bar and a couple of cocktail magicians shaking gold-plated shakers like crazy. They strain colourful and refreshing creations into what seems like a unique piece of crystal glassware for every drink. They look so good that I found myself watching what other people were ordering and asking if I could try that next. Optional snacks are floating around the bar and sliders and skewer-style dishes can be called upon from the kitchen. But if you really want to get that stomach lined for the evening, the booze-infused fondue (aged cheddar and mescal) really caught my attention. The decorative hexagon pattern on the wall pays homage to a beehive. It might also have something to do with the way patrons interact with the space – buzzing in and out into the series of the more secluded booth-style seating options.

18 LATIN AMERICAN CLUB

3286 22nd St
415 647 2732
Open Mon–Fri 5pm–2am,
Sat–Sun 12pm–2am
[MAP p. 187 E4]

The decor here is what I can only describe as a cowboy-themed bar that once had a birthday party and never took the now sun-bleached piñatas down. With cuckoo clocks, giant swordfish and letterboxes mounted on the wall, I can only imagine the sounds that might reverberate through that top room. Very few times have I been handed a single drink that was so full of value – the margarita I drank in here was flooring. For $15 I was sorted for over an hour. I'm also told that from 5–7pm there is $1 off everything.

FIELD TRIP

EAST BAY: OAKLAND & BERKELEY

East Bay comprises a series of smaller cities that offer a less hectic, more down-to-earth vibe than San Francisco. The affordable housing and relatively quick train trip into the city makes the area appealing for locals looking to commute, and it makes for a much more relaxed and affordable place for visitors to stay, shop, eat and drink.

Oakland's Downtown is the central business district (CBD) and often encompasses Chinatown and Civic Centre, too. You can explore a range of unique nightlife in Downtown (see p. 132), take a stroll around Lake Merritt (see p. 132) and indulge in some crafty shopping and special foodie experiences in neighborhoods like Temsecal and Piedmont (see p. 132). Jack London Square is the main marina-style entertainment precinct, with a huge range of eateries and entertainment. It's a nice strip to go for a stroll when you don't really know exactly what you are looking for. Downtown Oakland is accessible from San Francisco by BART (train) stops at both 12th and 19th street stations, which can be as little as a 20-minute ride from central San Francisco.

Further north from Oakland is Berkeley, which has famously been a site of social and political change within the United States. It is the birthplace of the free-speech movement, later a thriving scene for anarchists-cum-punks and more recently home to black bloc activists. Downtown Berkeley (see p. 135) is home to a range of great food and drink options. It's a hive of both academics and creatives, and the University of California (UC) Berkeley campus – the flagship of the UC group. It's a short journey from San Francisco, with several attractions well worth the visit. If you have the chance to stay near Downtown, Berkeley is easily accessible from San Francisco by public transport or via a short drive over the Bay Bridge.

→ Rasputin Music, Berkeley

POCKET TIP

In Uptown Oakland, a short trip north on Broadway, are the Fox (1807 Telegraph Ave) and Paramount (2025 Broadway) theatres. Both have fantastic Art Deco designs and it's well worth seeing a show.

GRAND LAKE

HAND COUNTED PAPER BALLOTS
ARE THE ONLY PATH TO ENDING THE
HACKING THEFT OF OUR ELECTIONS!

DOWNTOWN OAKLAND & LAKE MERRITT

In Downtown Oakland, clustered around **Jack London Square**, you'll find a range of creative joints in which to eat and drink. I recommend **Café Van Clief** (1621 Telegraph Ave), famous for their greyhound cocktail, and **Small Wonder** (37 Grand Ave), an eccentrically decorated *Alice in Wonderland*–type eatery, sprawling over several levels.

Lake Merritt is a fantastic place to go for a stroll or a run on a sunny afternoon. It's the perfect spot to bring a few supplies and a picnic rug to spread out on the grass. The famous **Grand Lake theatre** stands at the entrance of Grand Avenue, where a handful of charming shops and dining halls are clustered. **Smitty's, Grand Tavern** and the **Libertine** are all top places to stop off for a bite to eat or a cocktail.

TEMESCAL, PIEDMONT & ROCKRIDGE SHOPPING & EATING

Temescal is home to several quaint little pedestrian shopping streets filled with a string of cool little independent stores that rotate regularly, selling plants, handmade jewellery and crafty soaps. To the other side is the **Temescal Brewery**

(4115 Telegraph Ave) – they're really serious about their beers and really serious about their community, hosting events like Queer First Fridays, they regularly support their LGBTQIA+ friends. They have also been known to donate a portion of sales to support related causes. **Betty Bakes** (5098 Telegraph Ave) serves some of the most sought-after chicken sandwiches and pies in the Bay Area. And they're made by Australians! The Piedmont Avenue neighbourhood is a strip known for dining and retail and famous **Fenton's** ice-creamery (4226 Piedmont Ave). There's a great tiki bar called the **Kona Club** (4401 Piedmont Ave) and a divey little cabin style bar called **The Lodge** (3758 Piedmont Ave) that sells cheap cans for the penny-rich punter.

Rockridge is charming and filled with a nice mixture of multicultural restaurants and crafty retail outlets. You'll notice open shopfronts with outdoor seating, bookshops and florists sprawling out onto the street. Rockridge sits on the fringe of Berkeley and is certainly the more affluent end of the area. There's a stylish collection of cafes and upmarket restaurants, too. On the way from Temescal to Rockridge, you'll hit **Kingfish** (5227 Telegraph Ave), one of my favourite pubs to play shuffleboard. Get involved!

133

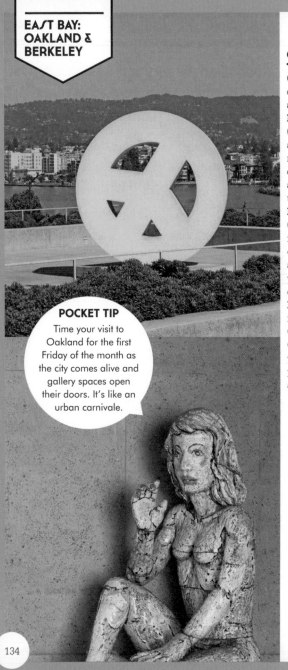

EAST BAY: OAKLAND & BERKELEY

POCKET TIP

Time your visit to Oakland for the first Friday of the month as the city comes alive and gallery spaces open their doors. It's like an urban carnivale.

OAKLAND MUSEUMS

Oakland is home to a series of interesting museums and attractions. The **Oakland Museum of California** (1000 Oak St) is filled with a collection of art history, natural science and interactive displays. For something a bit more obscure, visit the **Museum of Art and Digital Entertainment** (3400 Broadway) to completely immerse yourself in the creativity behind gaming, and even play a game or two yourself. Or for a more elevated experience, the **Aviation Museum** (8252 Earhart Rd) is filled with classic aircraft. At **Chabot Space and Science Centre** (10000 Skyline Blvd) you can engage with a planetarium, telescopes and all things space related.

BERKELEY SHOPPING & EATING

Around Downtown Berkeley station you'll find a cohort of vegan restaurants and Tibetan gift stores, lingering from the hippie days. Populated by a combination of college kids and trendy locals, they keep good business.

Shattuck Avenue is the major street in East Bay running all the way through to Oakland. It's plotted with top spots to eat and drink, including several major cultural institutions, such as **BAMPFA** (2155 Center St), the university's art gallery and film archive.

My personal favourite eatery is **Jupiter** (2181 Shattuck Ave), a wood-oven pizza joint, with its own brews on tap and large plates of wings – perfect for late nights inside or boozy afternoons relaxing in the very green beer garden. For excellent but semi-upmarket Mexican fare, heading to **Comal** is a great option. **Saturn** (2175 Allston Way) cafe is a reliable place for vegan diner delights. **Tupper and Reed** (2271 Shattuck Ave) is a great spot to grab a world-class cocktail. If a casual beer is more your thing, there's no shortage of watering holes in the area. **Triple Rock Brewing** (1920 Shattuck Ave) and **Revival Bar** (2102 Shattuck Ave) are

135

two I've visited regularly. Heading away from Downtown is the **Art House Gallery & Cultural Center** (2905 Shattuck Ave).

On football game days, the entire university area turns up and does the whole American college movie thing with 'Go Bears' (the university football team). It's quite an experience wandering through the university grounds, checking out the historic architecture. I particularly enjoy strolling along Telegraph Avenue, which has a few pretty stellar shops to visit. Kind of like a mini Haight-Ashbury (see p. 26); you'll find a group of the coolest record stores, such as **Rasputin** (2401 Telegraph Ave) and **Amoeba** (2455 Telegraph Ave). There's also some decent vintage shops, like **Anastasia** (2360 Telegraph Ave), **Mars** (2398 Telegraph Ave) and the **T-Shirt Orgy** (2350 Telegraph Ave). There are glittering old-school silver screen theatres, such as **The Elmwood** (2966 College Ave), which is a little further out

but regularly plays indie and foreign films in an old theatre filled with retro decor.

Alcatraz Avenue is the cool-kid street, with the main cluster of good locations on the corner of Alcatraz Avenue and Adeline Street. Here you'll find boutique vintage shops, great Cajun food at **Easy Creole**, **Alchemy Coffee**, **Hercules** records and **Hoi Polloi Taphouse**, with a set of rotating taps and free popcorn. There's regular street parties on the weekends, too.

OUTDOOR/

Berkeley Hills and **Tilden National Park** offer a range of short hikes for both the beginner and intermediate hiker, including **Grizzly Peak** – a nice spot to take in a sunset while you look at **Mount Diablo** in the distance. Other great outdoor localities include hiking through **Tilden Regional Park**, swimming in **Lake Anza** and climbing at **Indian Rock**. Closer in, both the **Berkeley Marina** and the **Rose Garden** make for a lovely afternoon stroll if you're looking for something more relaxing to do.

FIELD TRIP

ƒANTA CRUZ &
THE COAƒT

Highway 1 is a fantastically accessible way to tour the beautiful Californian coastline. There's a seriously great range of different activities and unique turn-offs along the way. It's perfect if you're living the van life or renting an RV.

Marin County commences just as you cross the Golden Gate Bridge, north out of San Francisco, and includes the picturesque Marin Headlands (*see* p. 140), quaint Sausalito (*see* p. 140), Bolinas villages (*see* p. 141), Mount Tamalpais (*see* p. 141) for hiking and Stinson Beach (*see* p. 141).

Santa Cruz (*see* p. 143) is a beach town, south of San Francisco, with popular wharfside attractions and a history of surf culture. Many iconic labels have grown out of the area – you might know it for the famous skateboard/surf brand with the same name. Be sure to visit both the Boardwalk (*see* p. 143) and the Surfing Museum (*see* p. 144). The area is in close quarters to a range of famous surf beaches and redwood forests.

Santa Cruz can be accessed using a combination of public transport, such as CalTrain (*see* p. 162), which takes around three hours from San Francisco and costs approximately $25. Driving takes about an hour and a half.

→ Looking at the wharf from West Cliff Drive

MARIN HEADLANDS & SAUSALITO

The **Marin Headlands** are pretty phenomenal and potentially the most spectacular vantage point from which to see the **Golden Gate Bridge**, and it is also the site of an old military base and a bunch of exceptionally exclusive artist's studios. You have the option of riding a bike to the headlands over the Golden Gate Bridge, which can be worth it considering the traffic (especially on weekends). **Sausalito**, the first town you hit going over the bridge, is a quaint town on the opposite shore to Marina District and far more relaxing than anything you'll find on the other side of the bay. It's a great place to have a meal of fresh seafood at **Scoma's Sausalito** (588 Bridgeway) on the pier, get some waterfront shopping done or sit and take in the marina views that overlook the large houseboat community. You can arrange bike riding, sailing and seaplane charters that depart from the area, too. You can catch a chartered ferry to Sausalito from San Francisco. Sausalito has easy access to the surrounding wilderness areas, like **Muir Woods** (*see* p.141) and **Mount Tamalpais** (*see* p.141), and it is a fantastic place to see the **Golden Gate Bridge** with city views in the background.

BOLINAS, MOUNT TAMALPAIS & STINSON BEACH

Bolinas is a fantastic place to get out of San Francisco for a few days and stay in a cosy bed and breakfast or coastal shack. It's a somewhat hidden place, only accessible by windy backroads and unsealed paths, giving it a reclusive kind of feel. This coastal community boasts charming little villages with some seriously lovely coastline just around the corner. Downtown Bolinas claims to have the oldest general store and one of the oldest gas stations in the United States.

East of Bolinas, you'll find **Stinson Beach**, a sprawling sandy parcel perfect for days on deck chairs and sunbathing. It's close to some excellent hiking for both experienced and amateur hikers in **Muir Woods** and **Mount Tamalpais**, both of which are located in preserved parks filled with numerous trailheads. From the summit of Mount Tamalpais, you'll see views of the ocean and the city with fog rolling in from every direction. The park opens at 7am and closes at sunset. You'll need $8 cash to get in. There's a range of different trails accessible that commence from different points.

141

NICK'S COVE, TOMALES BAY & BODEGA BAY

Further along the coast past **Point Rayes National Park**, you'll come across one of my favourite destination dining spots, just a short (ish) 1.5 hour drive from San Francisco. **Nick's Cove** (23240 CA-1, Marshall), dined at by many a celebrity over the years, offers a very unique experience: the opportunity to dine out in a boathouse at the end of a jetty. You can order in fish and chips from the payphone inside and get a personalised kit to make s'mores in winter. Further along the coast, you'll hit **Tomales Bay**. Sit on the beach and buy yourself an exceptionally cheap dozen oysters to shuck (yes, yourself). I'd suggest bringing a glove, but the fishermen will lend you the knife. At popular times there's a drinks cart, too. **Bodega Bay**, the next stop along, has a selection of nice cafes and seafood eateries. There's also plenty of locations for kayaking, paddle boarding and coastal hiking.

⨯ANTA CRUZ BOARDWALK

POCKET TIP
There are some fun detours en route from San Francisco to Santa Cruz, such as San Jose, Silicon Valley and Stanford University.

The Boardwalk runs along the coast of Monterey Bay. A collection of souvenir stores, bars and restaurants run along the opposite side of the beach. On the beach side, you'll find sunbathers, sandcastle building, volleyball players and a few oceanside bars. The wharf is an iconic walking strip home to fishing and sea lions and for spotting sunsets. There's a range of places to casually grab a glass of wine and some fish and chips, like **Woodies Café** or **FireFish Grill**. Further around from the pier, you'll hit all kinds of fun along the **Santa Cruz Beach Boardwalk**. Founded in 1907, it's California's oldest amusement park. Test yourself at **Neptune's Kingdom**, an indoor video game arcade filled with family favourites old and new. Just around the corner is your chance to play miniature golf, and ride the **Giant Dipper Roller Coaster** and the **Looff Carousel**, both of which are considered national landmarks.

143

Many local surfers were called to service during World War II. Even though surfing activity slowed, locals on leave surfed when home and many "out of towners" stationed at Fort Ord, Alameda, Treasure Island, and the Presidio came to Santa Cruz to surf during off-duty hours and borrowed the locals' boards. By the late 40s and early 50s the members of the Santa Cruz Surfing Club had married and started families that required full-time jobs and left little time for surfing. So they turned the beach and the waves over to a new generation of surfers.

SANTA CRUZ SURFING CLUB
JUNE, 1941

SURFING MUSEUM

701 W Cliff Dr, Santa Cruz
831 420 6289
Open Thurs–Mon 12pm–4pm
[MAP p. 181 D2]

An enjoyable walk from the Boardwalk (see p. 143), where you can also spot some surfing in action, is the Santa Cruz Surfing Museum. You can't miss it – it's in the unique location at the base of the lighthouse. The museum has memorabilia and archives from the very first time surfing ever occurred in the United States. You'll see photographs, vintage memorabilia and learn about the local surf legends, like Duke Kahanamoku and Jack O'Neill. You can explore the exciting history of surfing in the United States and see how the sport has changed and evolved over the years from the native Hawaiian mode to beachside competitions with crowds and global brand sponsorship.

POCKET TIP
Like all Californian cities, there's many Airbnbs and major hotels in Santa Cruz. Due to its proximity to nature, there's a range of great campsites and RV parks, too.

POCKET TIP

Penny Ice-Creamery (913 Cedar St) is an absolute Santa Cruz must, always with queues. Try flavours like bourbon bacon chocolate and salted butter toffee, but the menu changes with seasonal local produce.

MY/TERY /POT

465 Mystery Spot Rd, Santa Cruz
831 423 8897
www.mysteryspot.com
Open Mon–Fri 10am–4pm,
Sat–Sun 10am–5pm
[MAP p. 181 D2]

Prepare to question your own beliefs surrounding gravity. This unusual experience a few kilometres outside Santa Cruz is a must-see when visiting the area. The mystery spot is 'a gravitational phenomenally', situated amongst the giant redwoods. You'll be amazed as you enter an area where physics no longer seem to make sense. During the 45-minute guided tour you'll be puzzled seeing golf balls roll up hills, and be questioning how your friend is falling over as they stand at a 90 degrees angle on a table (like something from the *Exorcist*). Booking in advance is recommended.

145

NAPA VALLEY

Napa Valley, often synonymous with Californian wine, ritzy getaways and the wealthy elite, is about an hour's drive north of San Francisco. You may recognise the name from your local bottle shop, perhaps you've stumbled across movies like *Sideways*, *Bottleshock* or more recently *Wine Country*. Funny as they are, the basics of them aren't far from the truth. Napa is a place for wine tasting (*see* p. 148) and to sample local produce at places such as Oxbow Public Market (*see* p. 150).

Napa County and the Valley within are comprised of a series of small towns. Famous names like Calistoga, Yountville and St Helena are just a few that stand out as destinations. Amongst them are literally hundreds of vineyards, tasting rooms and accommodation options. Downtown Napa is a good place to stay with access to a bit of everything.

You can get to the Napa Valley one of several ways. Firstly, and most conveniently by rental car/driving. Secondly, by taking a ferry from the Ferry Building (*see* p. 2) in San Francisco to Vallejo and then taking an Uber rideshare or bus to Downtown Napa Valley. Thirdly, there is a shuttle bus from the airport. Although Napa can be done as a daytrip from San Francisco, I'd suggest at least two, if not three, days to get a fuller experience.

→ *Vineyards in St Helena*

WINE TASTING

You might visualise wine tasting as a casual and affordable (often free) experience. I would remove those illusions when talking about Napa Valley. It's a world of prestige, and you can expect to pay $30 to $100 per person to be taken on tours around lavish grounds, all of which should be booked over the phone or online beforehand. You'll be transported to some majestic locations with cellar staff that know their stuff. Expect terms like soft tannin, high viscosity and Brettanomyces to be thrown around like it's no big deal. I wouldn't plan on doing more than two or three locations per day, otherwise it's going to cost you and you'll feel rushed. While there are more than 400 wineries to visit, here's a few stand-out experiences:

Opus One (Oakvale, en.opusonewinery.com) is the brainchild of two of the most famous wine families in the world – Rothschild and Mondavi. Once rated the most expensive wine in California, the pristine vineyards and lavish estate, in harmony with the vineyards surrounding it, are quite a surreal experience.

Beringer (St Helena, www.beringer.com) was founded in 1876 and is said to be the longest-running, continually operated winery in the valley.

Tastings are broken into reds, whites and museum releases, which are perhaps the most affordable.

At **Castello di Amorosa** (Calistoga, castellodiamorosa. com) the wine isn't as renowned, but it comes served in the dungeon of an Italian eccentric's modern-made replica 13th-century Tuscan castle.

The **Wine Train** (www.winetrain.com) is a pretty extraordinary experience. You sit in restored early 20th-century Pullman carriages as you travel from Downtown Napa to St Helena, admiring the scenery along the way. Seasonal food is served for lunch and dinner (anyone for a four-course meal?), there are optional stop-offs and wine tasting is included. See the website for special tours and events, too.

OXBOW PUBLIC MARKET

Oxbow is my favourite part of Napa Valley. An open-setting market comparable to the Ferry Building (*see* p. 2) in San Francisco. It takes all the awesome elements of the region and puts them under one roof. You'll find all kinds of produce – pick your cut of local meat and have it cooked right in front of you at **Five Dot**, which runs a special natural beef program, creating the most incredible produce that's both antibiotic- and hormone-free. Enjoy your cut with sides, as a sandwich or take it to your accommodation to cook. Enjoy some fresh oysters from **Hog Island**, harvested and delivered daily from Tomales Bay (*see* p. 142), on the coast of northern California. Try a fantastic cup of coffee at **Ritual Coffee Roasters**, one of San Francisco's original third-wave coffee roasters. You'll find regular coffee options as well as a more artisanal range, and you should sit down and enjoy the experience to take a break from walking. Sample some of

Fieldworks hop-forward draughts; originally founded in Berkeley, Fieldwork has become a local favourite within the Bay Area. Grab one of the classic burgers and fries from **Gott's Roadside**. Gott's is a family owned burger chain unique to northern California. It specialises in using inventive and fresh ingredients throughout its entire range. Personally, I'm a fan of the Green Chile cheeseburger, with a side of garlic fries and an Arnold Parmer beer.

151

DOWNTOWN NAPA

There is a decent list of great food and drink joints in Downtown Napa; these tend to operate rather late and pick up quite a crowd. You could potentially visit Napa and spend your entire time here, as there is enough to do. A favourite of mine is **Blue Note** (1030 Main St), a legitimate Manhattan-style jazz bar with live music and top-notch cocktails in a dimly lit atmosphere, open most nights of the week. **Downtown Joes** (902 Main St) is a restaurant/brewery and home to a country-style party vibe after 9pm. Purveyors of cold beer, good happy hours and confronting karaoke performances. The **Bounty Hunter** (975 1st St) serves low and slow barbecue until late and a pours a great selection of full-bodied reds by the glass and tasting flight. **Morimoto** (610 Main St) is a silver service restaurant with really memorable Japanese fare.

RUSSIAN RIVER BREWERY

725 4th St, Santa Rosa
russianriverbrewing.com
Open Mon–Sun 11am–12am
(kitchen closes 11pm)

Russian River is not exactly in Napa Valley, but I wanted to mention this location, firstly, because **Santa Rosa** is a great little town with some excellent camping and coast nearby, but also because the taphouse alone is seriously worth the visit. The 50-barrel production brewery has potentially the largest tasting flight in the world offering a whopping 18-glass sampler that can be accompanied by crispy wood-oven pizzas. Home to beers like Pliny and Blind Pig, this famous microbrewery is credited with inventing the double IPA and fathering the sour/lambic beer movement within the region.

YOSEMITE NATIONAL PARK

Located in California's Sierra Nevada mountains, Yosemite is one of the world's most renowned national parks. Filled with giant ancient sequoia trees, iconic viewpoints, sweeping landscapes and monumental granite rock formations, it's certainly a place to be remembered. Away from the centre of the range, the landscape begins to merge into sprawling meadows, open plains, quaint towns and even wine regions.

Yosemite's remarkable landscapes have been the inspiration for the branding behind the outdoor label North Face, the basis of epic film documentaries, an array of award-winning photographic exhibitions and even prompted the titles of Apple's software updates.

Hike or backpack in the High Sierra, and snowboard or ski (*see* p. 160) the parks or kayak the Merced River (*see* p. 158). There is no shortage of activities to consider. Check out Half Dome (*see* p. 157 and p. 161), Yosemite's iconic climbing face, watch the sun come down over El Capitan (*see* p. 157), take in the lookout over Glacier Point (*see* p. 157) and feel the sheer pressure behind the waterfalls (*see* p. 161).

Yosemite is home to a huge range of wildlife – some you want to run into and some you don't. Particularly American Black Bears! It's important to take note of signage and have an action plan if you see a bear, remaining at a minimum of 15 metres (50 feet) away. Bears generally want to avoid people too, and are just looking for easy access to food. Use the bear-safe disposal bins to throw away scraps and keep all food in the provided storage lockers, where possible. Be sure to keep all food stored in your car out of sight and avoid leaving it out in the open, even within plastic containers. It is illegal to feed any animals in the park, so if you come across any friendly critters, keep your food away.

→ *El Capitan and beyond*

155

GETTING TO YO/EMITE

You can drive to Yosemite from San Francisco directly in around three hours. Use a combination of highways: I-580 before getting on I-5 southbound from there, but use a GPS – trust me. You'll need to purchase a parks pass, which costs $20 per vehicle and can be bought at several entrance stations. **Grayline** bus tours are an affordable option from San Francisco but ensure that you will have access to some of the public transport and shuttles offered within Yosemite when you book accommodation. **Valley Floor** guided bus tours can also be a simple choice upon arrival if you're looking for an organised way to see the highlights.

The time of year that you head to Yosemite will affect the kind of activities you'll do and the kind of experience you'll have. In spring, you'll see dramatic waterfalls and blooming flowers; in winter, the ski parks will be open; summer can be warm and there will be plenty of others on vacation, too; autumn is less busy, and the crowds will fall off – it's a pleasant climate for hiking and daytrips, but it can be wet so bring that poncho.

/IGHT/

Spectacular vistas and walks are what Yosemite is famed for. If you're a more serious and experienced hiker, *see* p. 160.

El Capitan is a popular rock climbing face, found on the north side of Yosemite Valley. This 2307-metre (7569-foot) granite monolith can be admired in the distance or, for the avid adventurer, hiked to the top. **Half Dome** is another epic and obscure-shaped piece of granite on the eastern edge of the valley, at 2694 metres (4800 feet) and can also be hiked (*see* p. 161) via the heart-stopping **Cable Route**. **Tunnel View** is a hike-free experience within the park and considered by many as one of the most awe-inspiring and easily accessible vistas on offer. The view encompasses El Capitan, Half Dome and **Bridalveil Fall**. The viewing platform is located within the valley, just outside Wawona Tunnel on State Highway 41. **Glacier Point** is on the southern wall of the valley and offers a different, vaster panoramic of the surrounding rock formations and wilderness. **Tuolumne Meadows**, with the Tuolumne River running through it, is in the eastern area of the national park. The windy streams and lush wetlands make for a fantastic photograph at sunrise and sunset. For the less rugged

traveller or for that welcome day off, Yosemite offers a plethora of other activities, including **ranger talks** nightly around a campfire and the **Ansel Adams Gallery** (9031 Village Dr), filled with pioneering photography of the region. You can even go kayaking on the **Merced River**. There are a range of adventure companies offering guided tours and rental services that can be found within the village or online.

SLEEPING

If you want to be close to all of the action and the major attractions, staying within the valley is a good idea but book ahead – especially in busy periods. If you plan on only spending a day in the park, staying within the valley and visiting the village is probably your best option. The village is equipped with grocery store, souvenir shops and even a post office. From this area accessing all of the major attractions like **Half Dome** (*see* p. 157) and **El Capitan** (*see* p. 157) is quite achievable. You'll also be in close proximity to a series of self-guided hikes. If you have a bit more time in the area, you might like to look into some extended activities that suit your particular interests, such as skiing or snowboarding in winter (*see* p. 160). Yosemite has 13 listed campgrounds.

Facilities and prices vary from location to location, and some campsites do not allow RVs, so it pays to assess your options online before departing – check the **National Parks Service** website (www.nps.gov/yose). There's also a large range of more established accommodation options, from the glamourous **Majestic Yosemite Hotel** that was built in the 1920s, to some more affordable options like the **Yosemite Valley Lodge** and **Half Dome Village** tent cabins. There are a range of Airbnb options that are in close proximity to the major attractions, but once again, be sure to consider nearby transport options if you do not have access to a vehicle.

EATING

The **Majestic Yosemite Hotel** offers an exceptional dining experience amongst high wooden ceilings and cathedral-style windows, serving an intriguing mix of upmarket American cuisine. The **Yosemite Valley Lodge** has both the mountain room, offering spectacular views, and a more casual food court. Half Dome Village has a range of affordable food options, including **Pizza Pavilion** and **Meadows Grill**.

POCKET TIP

The national parks pass gives you access to various national parks near San Francisco and Los Angeles, such as Kings Canyon, Death Valley and Joshua Tree. See www.usparkpass.com

SKIING & CLIMBING

During the winter season (December to March), the **Badger Pass Ski Area** is open for business. There are perfect slopes for all grades of snowboarders and skiers and a school for beginners. Gear is available to hire, and there are both full- and half-day lift passes available that can be purchased on the site. Yosemite has become a major climbing attraction over the years, and you'll often see climbers on **Half Dome** (*see* p. 157) and the other faces during your visit. For non-locals and travellers alike, stick with the professionals from **Yosemite Mountaineering School & Guide Service** (9020 Curry Village Dr), which offers both lessons and gear hire for a range of different styles and skill levels.

HIKING

Ranging from 1–26 kilometres (0.6–16 miles) and varying in difficulty from easy to strenuous, there will be a walk or hike that suits your ability. **Yosemite Valley Loop Trail** is a nice option with few undulations, designed for moderate hikers. The trail is 21 kilometres (13 miles) and takes between five and seven hours. There is also a half loop alternative that only takes half the time.

Cathedral Lakes and **Mono Pass** are both under 12 kilometres (7.5 miles) and can be done within an afternoon. These walks are moderate and easy enough for beginner hikers. **Half Dome Hike** is around 22–26 kilometres (14–16 miles) and is for a more advanced hiker. You'll need a permit to do this hike and it will take the best part of the day. **El Capitan** can also be hiked and is considered a similar degree of difficulty to Half Dome. It's approximately 20 kilometres (12 miles) and usually takes a day to complete. Both the **Bridalveil Fall** hike and the **Mist Trail** are under 4.8 kilometres (3 miles) and can be done easily in one or two hours if you are fit. During the right season, Yosemite is famous for its waterfalls and the surrounding hikes, which include **Lower Yosemite Falls**, **Vernal Falls** and **Nevada Falls**.

TRAVEL TIPS

GETTING TO SAN FRANCISCO

Flying

San Francisco International Airport (SFO) is the primary transit route when flying in. Set only 21 kilometres (13 miles) from downtown, it's quite conveniently located. The airport is the seventh most visited airport in the United States (24th in the world) and the largest in northern California. It is comprised of three domestic terminals and an international airport. There is a continuously rotating museum exhibit for something interesting to do while you wait, right in the middle of the terminal! There are lockers, unlike at other American airports, to store luggage if required.

Dedicated taxi zones exist and a taxi will cost you around $45 to the city, but I would recommend rideshares Lyft and Uber (see p. 163), the pick-up locations will be apparent with the app. BART (Bay Area Rapid Transit) trains run directly to the city on the Millbrae line, and Clipper Cards or day tickets can be purchased at the airport.

Oakland International Airport (OAK) can on occasion be a useful substitute for more convenient connections – particularly for domestic flights. OAK is an affordable rideshare-ride from Downtown San Francisco.

Train

Travelling between San Francisco and Los Angeles, you might decide to use the **CalTrain** (www.caltrain.com), an affordable and scenic option. However, it takes 11 hours, compared to a bus that takes seven and a half (see p. 162) and a car that takes six hours.

The **Amtrak** (www.amtrak.com) train runs from Los Angeles to Oakland and San Jose and offers a connection to San Francisco. Amtrak lines also run to and from Portland with an average duration of 16 hours, and then onto Seattle in around 22 hours. These depart from San Francisco's Montgomery BART station.

Travelling from other parts of the Bay Area and northern California can be done quickly, also using the CalTrain system.

Car

California is home to some of the world's most famous road trips, the famous coastal drives; Highway 1, the Pacific Northwest and the 49-Mile Scenic drive, just to name a few. These roadside adventures can be a great way to enter the Bay Area.

Driving to San Francisco from Los Angeles can be done conveniently in a day. Driving Highway 1 takes around nine hours and encounters some of the best scenery you'll ever see out of the window of a car. Driving Interstate 5 can take as little as six hours, but you better have some podcasts to keep you occupied. Highway 101 offers a combination of some of the scenery and a duration that falls somewhere in the middle.

From Portland or Seattle, Pacific Coast Highway and Highway 101 offer a longer drive but endless list of national parks and coastal sites on the trip through to San Francisco. This can take anything from 13 hours to a week depending on your detours. The I-5 offers the most direct route.

Driving tips

When driving within the United States, please consider that road rules will differ from your origin country and on occasion even between US states. In North America, you drive on the right side of the road. You'll need to know what to do at a four-way stop sign, and the DMV of California (www.dmv.ca.gov) has a drivers handbook available online. I'd personally also watch a few YouTube videos before you hop behind the wheel.

Depending on what country you are travelling from, you may be required to get an International Drivers Permit (IDP) first, which you'll need to get before you leave your own country. Check your travel insurance, too, to ensure you'll be covered for car hire and driving.

Bus

This can be an incredibly cheap option, however, not always the most comfortable. **Megabus** (www.megabus.com) runs from Los Angeles Union Station to San Francisco (corner of Townsend and 5th streets). There is a range of other bus services operating similar routes, the trip takes seven and a half hours and can be as cheap as $20.

GETTING AROUND SAN FRANCISCO

Rideshare

Rideshare platforms were born in this city, so naturally, you have a lot of options. **Lyft** and **Uber** are the most common. You'll be required to download the relevant app and sign up to the service first. Unless you have signed up to this before you leave your own country, you will require a local phone number. To save money on long trips, I would suggest considering **Uber Pool** or **Lyft Line**. This allows you to split the price with other passengers.

Remember tipping in an Uber is not required; you can choose to do so through the app if you want. A new app for females **Safr** provides a higher level of safety and vetting for drivers, allowing you to specify a female driver if you wish.

When using rideshare, consider surge pricing during peak periods. Also, consider airport charges.

Trains

The **Bay Area Rapid Transit system (BART)** is comprised of eight separate train lines running throughout San Francisco and the surrounding Bay Areas. BART operates both above and underground lines and stations. Lines are easy to navigate and operate quite regularly.

Although there are several useful and central stations in San Francisco, the geographic coverage can be limited. So travelling in conjunction with Muni (*see* below) light rail or bus system can be required. BART is convenient for travelling through to Oakland and Berkeley.

BART runs on the Clipper Card, which you can purchase at any station. You simply tap on and off. Fare prices can be as low as $2 and as high as $15, depending on how far you travel and what time of day.

Note that with BART vending machines, credit cards are limited to two transactions per 24-hour period, so make sure to top up your pass with sufficient amounts to meet your travel plans.

Buses & light rail

Muni buses and light rail metro trains cover all corners of the city. This system is far more comprehensive than BART within the precincts covered in this book.

Muni also operates on the Clipper Card system; you can also opt to pay cash onboard or use the MuniMobile app.

Historic streetcars and iconic cable cars are operated by Muni too, however, these can be a little more expensive, slower going and come with large queues during the busy periods.

MEDIA & TOURIST INFORMATION

There are several locations around San Francisco for general information, to book tours and to buy tickets.

The **Ferry Building** (*see* p. 2) has a tourism information booth, as does **Pier 39** (*see* p. 14). There is also a Downtown information centre at **749 Howard St**.

For further advice on food and drink beyond this book, I recommend:

www.sfgate.com/food

www.sfgate.com/entertainment

www.sfeater.com

www.liquor.com/mosaic/cityguides

http://cityguides.munchies.tv/city/san-francisco

To find upcoming music events and performances, I suggest heading to:

www.songkick.com/metro_areas/26330-us-sf-bay-area

www.bandsintown.com/en/c/san-francisco-ca

https://www.stubhub.com/sf-bay-area-tickets/geography/81/, which also includes sports and theatre.

TIME ZONES

The time zone in San Francisco is GMT-8. This is three hours behind New York City.

MONEY & ATMS

Cashpoints/ATMs are available throughout bank branches, corner stores and inside bars/restaurants. Fees are attached to these, so please look into this with your bank before you travel.

Contactless payment is less common in the United States than it is in Australia and the United Kingdom. However, phone payments and eWallet is available in more and more locations.

Your Visa, Mastercard and AMEX debit and credit services will work in most locations. Some places, such as hotels and car rental companies, will require credit and not a debit card.

Many establishments are cash only, and I would recommend checking before heading to an exact place if you don't want to carry money on you. Some may have ATMs inside and some may not. Cash is rarely required in retail outlets.

Remember to ensure you have the correct money to cover both tax and tips, this will not be included on the referenced price on the menu, learn more about typical foods here (see p. 166).

In general, unless you are in a flea market, the price is the price. Haggling is not a typical American custom.

PHONES

International code +1

Area code 415

If your phone is unlocked, you can use your existing mobile device. Global roaming can be an affordable option if used correctly, and some providers now offer fixed-day rates for usage, so it is worth checking in with yours before you travel.

Monthly contracts with large amounts of data are available for affordable prices from stores like Verizon and AT&T. This is a 5-minute seamless process.

Using data-based calling systems might also be a good option: Viber, Skype and Facebook all offer these services.

CLIMATE

San Francisco is rarely freezing cold or sweltering hot. It is often considered an idyllic climatic zone and is fairly consistent year round. There are cooler days in summer and warmer days that come in winter.

It rarely rains a lot even in the middle of winter, but there is a breeze that regularly comes in off the bay so having a softshell or light jacket in your pack is always a good idea. Year round, I would consider packing both a pair of jeans and a pair of shorts.

Summer: June to August – 11–20 degrees Celsius (51–68 degrees Fahrenheit)

Autumn: September to November – 12–17 degrees Celsius (54–63 degrees Fahrenheit)

Winter: December to February – 10–14 degrees Celsius (50–57 degrees Fahrenheit)

Spring: March to May – 9 –18 degrees Celsius (48–64 degrees Fahrenheit)

WI-FI

Wi-fi is generally provided for free in all Airbnbs, but it pays to check before booking. Hotels may charge for higher speed services but regularly offer a base option. Large chains like Mcdonalds and Starbucks generally offer free wi-fi.

The city has provided several convenient free wi-fi hotspots, too. See www.sfgov.org/sfc/sanfranciscowifi for a list of locations.

VOLTAGE & CONVERTERS

120V is the standard voltage in the United States. Please consider this before plugging in anything from countries like Australia and the United Kingdom. Your hairdryer may explode!

Merely having a plug converter will not fix this – you will require a step-down/step-up voltage converter. These can be quite costly, so consider this before buying appliances to bring back to your home country.

Appliances like phones and laptops, in general, are fine as the voltage/amp range is suitable for most countries with a pin convertor.

OPENING HOURS

General retail trading hours are 9/10am to 8/9pm. Corner stores are often open later until 11/12pm. Petrol/gas stations are not always open 24 hours, so it pays to be organised.

Restaurants often serve breakfast from 8 to 11 am, although some diners offer all-day breakfast. Lunch from 12pm to 2:30 pm is the regular service time. Dinner has several sittings ranging from around 5:30 to 9:30pm. There are all kinds of late-night food options around the city, typically diners and fast food offer later hours. Bars often operate until midnight and late night venues until 2am.

FESTIVALS

1 January New Year's Eve Fireworks Over the Bay – watch fireworks at The Embarcadero.

February Chinese New Year's Parade in Chinatown – celebrating the importance of Chinese culture and heritage in San Francisco.

April San Francisco International Film Festival – hundreds of films from over fifty countries presented over two weeks.

May Open Studios – a huge number of artists' works on display in an iconic naval shipyard.

June Pride Parade – a parade and festival celebrating the LGBTIQA+ community.

June–July Fillmore Jazz Festival – California's biggest free jazz festival.

June–August Stern Grove – concerts and a different artist each week for free amongst the trees in Sigmund Stern Grove, corner of 19th Avenue and Sloat Boulevard.

August Outside Lands – San Francisco's premier music and arts festival held in Golden Gate Park.

PUBLIC HOLIDAYS

New Year's Day 1 January

Martin Luther King Jr. Day 3rd Monday in January

Presidents' Day 3rd Monday in February. Not all states

Cesar Chavez Day 31 March

Memorial Day Last Monday in May

Independence Day 4 July

Labor Day 1st Monday in September

Veterans Day 12 November

Thanksgiving 4th Thursday in November

Day after Thanksgiving Day after 4th Thursday in November

Christmas Eve 24 December

Christmas Day 25 December

TIPPING

Tipping is generally required in restaurants offering table service. You should also tip your bartender in a bar. You do not have to tip both the restaurant host and your server. Tipping 15–20 per cent is standard; however, people often tip more if they enjoyed the service. If you're at a bar, I tend to leave a single dollar per drink.

Even if your meal was terrible, to not leave a tip at all is horrible behaviour. This would only be done if your meal didn't come at all or it was dropped in your lap.

You do not have to tip at take-away restaurants or fast food joints, although you can choose to.

You probably also should tip cab drivers, tour guides, a hotel bag person and the valet. You do not need to tip retail store clerks.

Keep your eye out when tipping, because some locations have a mandatory tip included. Do not feel compelled to go above and beyond this, unless you feel particularly well looked after.

If in doubt, just watch what other people are doing.

EATING & DRINKING

Taquerias & The Mission Burrito

The Mission-style burrito first became popular during the 1960s. Often referred to as a 'super burrito', some even trace its origins as far back as a protein-filled treat for the Central Valley fieldworkers of the 1930s. The Mission precinct (see p. 106) took a 'burrito' ('this little donkey'), and clicked the magnify button a few times – now taquerias cover every corner of the Bay Area – and serve the famous Mission burrito. The style is about softening a large tortilla to fit as much in as possible – meat, beans, rice, salsa and cheese. There's a range of different fillings specialised at each location. Regardless, it's large, wrapped in foil, easy to transport and simple to consume just about anywhere. It will last awhile in a backpack and covers every fundamental food group. It's easily modifiable to suit a range of tastes and dietary requirements, and it can be made as fancy or as basic as you want. It really is the peoples' food. You'll often find it sided by corn chips, with salsa and peppers from the counter – the custom is to add a little bit after each bite.

Class in a glass

At the Occidental Hotel in the mid-1800s, it's been said that Jerry Thomas (the Grandfather of all things cocktail) was earning $100 a week – more than the then Vice-President of the United States. The San Francisco bartender today is still a praised member of society and the cornerstone of every good night out.

Flour power

The distinctly tangy taste of sourdough and the chowder-filled bread bowls of Fisherman's Wharf aren't the only delights this city is getting all 'doughy-eyed' over. Whether you're having trouble finding a seat at a cafe exclusively serving toast or filling your tote bag with $9 country loaves from **Tartine** (see p. 122), don't be crumby – get yourself into a bakery.

Seafood

Despite the catastrophic oil spill in the '70s, populations of dungeness crab, clams, shrimp, scallops, squid and mussels are still pulled from the bay or close by. But what's an ingredient without a cook? Heading to **Swan Oyster Depot** (see p. 69) for a plate of Crab Louis or a Cioppino and chowder at **Tosca's** are just a couple of ways to enjoy the flavours of the sea.

Ice-cream

George Whitney invented the delicious ice-cream sandwich in 1928, the birthplace of **Swenson's**, often recognised as being the primary inspiration for Ben and Jerry's. Today ice-creameries across town are scooping flavours that keep the legacy alive. Find yourself a cup or cone on a sunny afternoon.

Coffee culture

Dating back to the gold rush, sourcing, roasting and brewing great coffee has always been a big part of San Francisco's blend. Famous names like Peets' and Trieste are still household names today. **Caffe Trieste** (see p. 8), imported the west-coast's first espresso in 1956. Today the booming third-wave of artisanal coffee providers are doing their forefathers proud, with a feverish focus on sourcing the right bean both ethically and sustainably, whilst mastering the techniques used to brew it. In the city with a million freelancers and flexible office hours, the humble coffee shop acts as the living room, the meeting place and the co-working space. Espresso, pour-over, siphon, filter or nitro; you'll be able to find it. A few brands you'll inevitably stroll past or seek out are: Ritual, Blue Bottle, Four Barrel and Sightglass.

Diners, dives & nostalgia

Neon signs, vinyl booths, dated jukeboxes, collections of clutter – these kind of places aren't made. Rather, they become – in a city that's seen earthquakes, flash fires, righteous movements and free love reign – an experience, a stalwart, an institution. We've covered a few examples of great diners and dives in this book. **Tommy's Joynt** (see p. 65), **Louis' Restaurant** (see p. 86), **Spec's Twelve Adler Museum Cafe** (see p. 9) and the **Tempest** (see p. 121) to name a few.

ACCOMMODATION

Like in any big city, there is a range of accommodation to suit all budgets. However, San Francisco accommodation can be expensive. The centre of San Francisco is home to just about every hotel chain imaginable. These tend to be located around Union Square and the general Marina area. Some are located on Market and The Embarcadero. These are ordinarily located near tourism information centres, car rentals and public transport.

Airbnb is undeniably the most popular option. Ranging from a tent in someone's backyard to a penthouse villa in Presidio Heights.

Hostels and dorms are available, although they can be of a low standard and can be expensive compared to other cities.

Monthly leases are an option in some states, including California. These can be a more affordable choice for stays over 30 days. Consider websites like: www.2ndaddress.com

While it is undeniably convenient to stay in the inner 7x7 San Francisco miles, simple transport options extend to the outer Bay Areas, which may be perfect for people that are mostly wanting to explore by day.

Van life can be an excellent option for those who need few comforts and want to travel beyond the city. A short drive outside San Francisco, particularly towards the coast and the national parks, an entire world of campsites and RV parks become available, filled with excellent facilities.

SECURITY & SAFETY

911 is the emergency response number within the United States.

553 0123 is the non-emergency number for San Francisco Police Department (SFPD).

San Francisco, like every big city, has its good and bad patches. The city is known for its homeless population, which is the third highest per capita in the United States after New York City and Los Angeles. In 2018, UN Special Rapporteur for Adequate Housing Lelani Farha reported on the San Francisco Bay region's housing crisis as a 'human rights violation', and many organisations are now looking for ways to improve the situation.

If you encounter any homeless people, remember they deserve respect like anyone else and have often found themselves homeless for reasons that are outside of their control. Most are safe to engage with but can be sketchy in the wrong situation, so use your common sense.

With tourism areas comes pickpockets and swindlers. Be cautious but don't be anxious – it's not a huge problem. Keep your valuables in a safe place, and don't flash them about in overcrowded or secluded areas.

If you are downtown at night be sure to catch an Uber or know your public transport options. These areas in particular should be travelled with caution: The Tenderloin, Potrero Hill, Twin Peaks, Dog Patch, Sunnydale and Bayview. This does not mean you can't stay visit here, just be savvy.

In general BART stations should not be lingered at at night unless necessary. If you must try to locate a place to wait, stand close to a guard or camera.

LEGAL MARIJUANA & DISPENSARIES

Purchasing marijuana is legal in California through registered retailers. This does not make it legal for purchase on the street, though.

You will need to be 21 years of age and provide your passport in order to make a purchase. If you choose to try marijuana but are not familiar with its effects, take it slow and don't consume too much too quickly.

Whilst legal, it's still not really okay to just stroll down The Embarcadero smoking a joint. It is illegal to smoke or eat cannabis in public spaces. It is also illegal to do so in places you cannot smoke cigarettes.

Do not drive if you're high. Just don't. It's a bad idea at the best of times, let alone in a crowded city you are unfamiliar with.

EMBASSIES

Australian Consulate
575 Market St
415 644 3620
Open Mon–Fri 9am-5pm

Consulate General New Zealand
This has shut down – the closest would be in Santa Monica or Los Angeles.

British Consulate General
1 Sansome St, Suite 850
415 617 1300
Open Mon–Fri 9am–4pm

Consulate General of Canada
580 California St #1400
415 834 3180
Open Mon–Fri 8:30am–4:30pm

B

C

1

GOLDEN
GATE
BRIDGE ⊕   Gate

Golden

192–3

2

BAKER
BEACH ⊕

*South
Bay*   PRESIDIO

LANDS
END

LANDS END
VIEWPOINT ⊕   ⊕ LEGION
OF HONOR   INNER
RICHMOND

SUTRO ⊕
BATHS   ○ LOUIS'
RESTAURANT

CLIFF ⊕
HOUSE   OUTER
RICHMOND

3

GOLDEN
GATE PARK   184–5

191

Pacific

Ocean   SAN   SUTRO
TOWER
⊕

FRANCISCO   TWIN
PEAKS

EUREKA & NOE
(MOUNTAIN PEAKS)

4

A   B   C

PARKSIDE

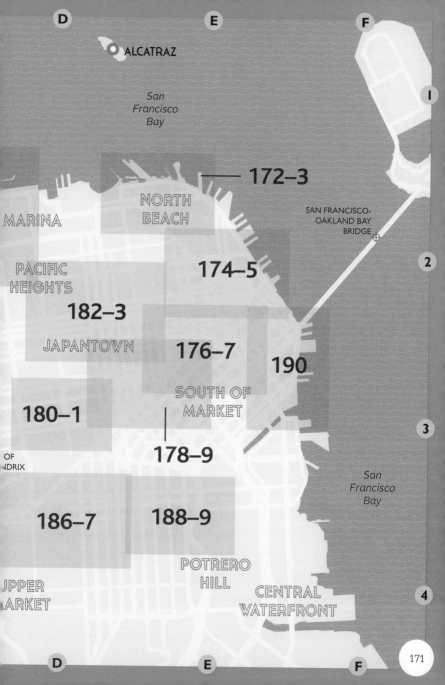

ALCATRAZ

San
Francisco
Bay

172–3

SAN FRANCISCO-
OAKLAND BAY
BRIDGE

MARINA

NORTH
BEACH

PACIFIC
HEIGHTS

174–5

182–3

JAPANTOWN

176–7

190

SOUTH OF
MARKET

180–1

OF
NDRIX

178–9

San
Francisco
Bay

186–7

188–9

JPPER
ARKET

POTRERO
HILL

CENTRAL
WATERFRONT

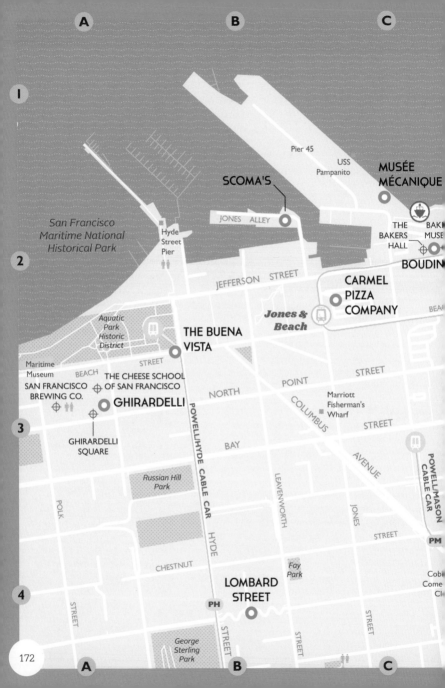

I

Pier 45

USS
Pampanito

MUSÉE
MÉCANIQUE

SCOMA'S

JONES ALLEY

THE
BAKERS
HALL

BAK
MUSE

San Francisco
Maritime National
Historical Park

Hyde
Street
Pier

BOUDIN

2

JEFFERSON STREET

CARMEL
PIZZA
COMPANY

BEAC

Jones &
Beach

Aquatic
Park
Historic
District

THE BUENA
VISTA

Maritime
Museum

BEACH STREET

SAN FRANCISCO
BREWING CO.

THE CHEESE SCHOOL
OF SAN FRANCISCO

GHIRARDELLI

POINT STREET

Marriott
Fisherman's
Wharf

3

GHIRARDELLI
SQUARE

NORTH

COLUMBUS

STREET

POWELL/HYDE CABLE CAR

BAY

POWELL/MASON CABLE CAR

POLK

Russian Hill
Park

LEAVENWORTH

AVENUE

JONES

STREET

PM

CHESTNUT

HYDE

Fay
Park

Cob
Come
Cl

4

STREET

LOMBARD
STREET

PH

STREET

STREET

George
Sterling
Park

SEA LION
VIEWING AREA

CANDY
BARON

BUBBA GUMP
SHRIMP CO.

*San
Francisco
Bay*

SAN
FRANCISCO
CAROUSEL

LEFTY'S
THE LEFT
HAND
STORE

*San
Francisco
Pier 41
Gate 1 & 2*

THE SAN
FRANCISCO
SOCK
MARKET

PIER 39

Pier 35

HARD
ROCK
CAFÉ

THE EMBARCADERO

Pier
33

STREET

HISTORIC STREETCARS

*Alcatraz
Cruises*

STREET

POINT

STREET

NORTH

FISHERMAN'S
WHARF

STREET

KEARNY

BAY

STOCKTON

N

STREET

POWELL

*Jack
Early
Park*

FRANCISCO

TELEGRAPH
HILL

0   200 m

STREET

GRANT

CHESTNUT

STREET

STREET

LOMBARD

NORTH
BEACH

PIONEER
PARK

*Joe DiMaggio
Playground*

AVENUE

TELEGRAPH HILL

COIT
TOWER

BLVD.

173

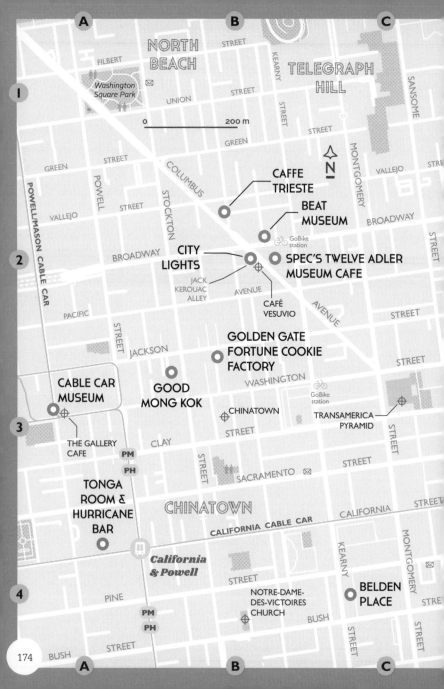

NORTH BEACH

STREET

KEARNY STREET

TELEGRAPH HILL

SANSOME STREET

FILBERT STREET

Washington Square Park

UNION STREET

200 m

GREEN STREET

MONTGOMERY STREET

VALLEJO

STRE

GREEN STREET

COLUMBUS

POWELL STREET

STOCKTON STREET

CAFFE TRIESTE

N

BEAT MUSEUM

GoBike station

BROADWAY

VALLEJO

BROADWAY

CITY LIGHTS

SPEC'S TWELVE ADLER MUSEUM CAFE

JACK KEROUAC ALLEY

AVENUE

CAFÉ VESUVIO

AVENUE

STREET

PACIFIC

JACKSON

STREET

GOLDEN GATE FORTUNE COOKIE FACTORY

STREET

CABLE CAR MUSEUM

GOOD MONG KOK

WASHINGTON

GoBike station

THE GALLERY CAFE

CHINATOWN

TRANSAMERICA PYRAMID

STREET

CLAY

STREET

PM

PH

TONGA ROOM & HURRICANE BAR

SACRAMENTO

CHINATOWN

STREET

CALIFORNIA CABLE CAR

CALIFORNIA

STREET

MONTGOMERY STREET

California & Powell

STREET

KEARNY STREET

PINE

PM

PH

NOTRE-DAME-DES-VICTOIRES CHURCH

BUSH

BELDEN PLACE

STRE

STREET

BUSH STREET

STREET

EXPLORATORIUM

Pier 15

Pier 9

Pier 7

FRONT STREET

GoBike station

THE EMBARCADERO

E F

San Francisco Bay

NORTHERN WATERFRONT

Sydney G. Walton Square

DAVIS STREET

JACKSON

GoBike station

COURT STREET

Gateway Theatre

WASHINGTON STREET

Ferry Park

Sue Bierman Park

HEATH CERAMICS

BLUE BOTTLE COFFEE

FLEA MARKETS

STREET

FRONT STREET

DAVIS STREET

GoBike station

Pier 3

Pier 1

Berkeley Ferry

BLUE BOTTLE COFFEE

GOTT'S ROADSIDE

THE SLANTED DOOR & OUT THE DOOR

Ferry Gate B

HOG ISLAND OYSTER CO.

Ferry Gates C & D

BOOK PASSAGE

Ferry Gate E

BOULETTES LARDER

GoBike station

FERRY BUILDING

TADICH GRILL

California & Davis

Embarcadero (subway)

Embarcadero (subway)

GoBike station

THE EMBARCADERO

E

BATTERY STREET

S

STREET

GoBike station

FREMONT STREET

BEALE STREET

MAIN STREET

MISSION STREET

SPEAR STREET

STEUART STREET

GoBike station

E T N

N M L K J F

MARKET

1ST STREET

FINANCIAL DISTRICT

SALESFORCE PARK

HOWARD STREET

STREET

D E F

D E F

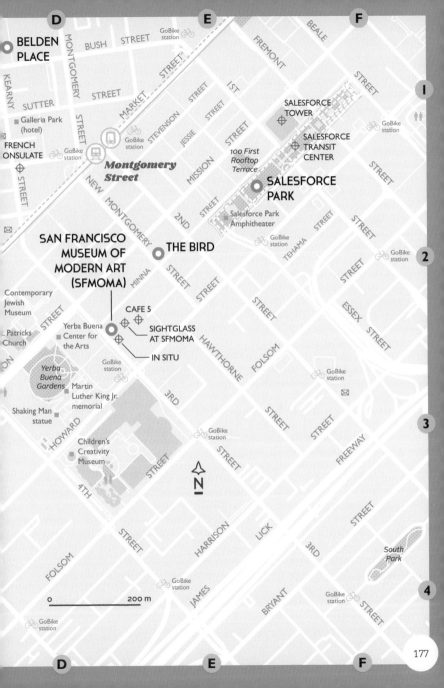

BELDEN PLACE

MONTGOMERY

BUSH STREET

GoBike station

E

BEALE

F

STREET

I

KEARNY

SUTTER

MARKET STREET

STREET

Galleria Park
(hotel)

MONTGOMERY STREET

GoBike station

Montgomery Street

GoBike station

STEVENSON

JESSIE

1ST STREET

STREET

STREET

FREMONT

SALESFORCE
TOWER

STREET

GoBike station

FRENCH
ONSULATE

STREET

NEW MONTGOMERY

MISSION STREET

100 First
Rooftop
Terrace

SALESFORCE
TRANSIT
CENTER

SALESFORCE
PARK

STREET

SAN FRANCISCO
MUSEUM OF
MODERN ART
(SFMOMA)

2ND STREET

THE BIRD

Salesforce Park
Amphitheater

GoBike station

STREET

GoBike station

2

Contemporary
Jewish
Museum

MINNA STREET

STREET

CAFE 5

TEHAMA

STREET

ESSEX STREET

Patricks
Church

Yerba Buena
Center for
the Arts

SIGHTGLASS
AT SFMOMA

IN SITU

HAWTHORNE

FOLSOM

ON

Yerba
Buena
Gardens

GoBike station

GoBike station

3

Martin
Luther King Jr.
memorial

STREET

FREEWAY

Shaking Man
statue

HOWARD

Children's
Creativity
Museum

3RD STREET

GoBike station

N

STREET

4TH STREET

HARRISON STREET

LICK

3RD STREET

South
Park

STREET

FOLSOM

0   200 m

GoBike station

JAMES

BRYANT STREET

GoBike station

STREET

4

GoBike station

D

E

F

177

A

B

C

SCOTT

STREET

WESTERN
ADDITION

Fillmore &
Turk Mini
Park

TURK

GATE

AVENUE

1

GOLDEN

Chateau Tivoli
Bed and Breakfeast

GoBike
station

FILLMORE

PIERCE

STREET

DIVISADERO

STREET

MCALLISTER

STEINER

STREET

N

EDDIE'S
CAFE

FULTON

STREET

The
Grove
Inn

STE

2

BAR
CRUDO

THE MILL

ALAMO
SQUARE

STREET

GROVE

STREET

PAINTED
LADIES

STREET

GROVE

GoBike
station

Alamo
Square
Playground

TOPO
DESIGNS

THE
INDEPENDENT

STREET

Casa L
(ho

HAYES

NOPA

ALAMO
SQUARE

STREET

3

FELL

STEINER

Church of
8 Wheels
(skate rink)

STREET

SCOTT

PIERCE

OAK

STREET

GoBike
station

LOWER
HAIGHT

200 m

STREET

0

BRODERICK

PAGE

GoBike
station

STREET

STREET

4

TORONAD

STREET

HAIGHT

LAUSSAT

STRE

A

B

C

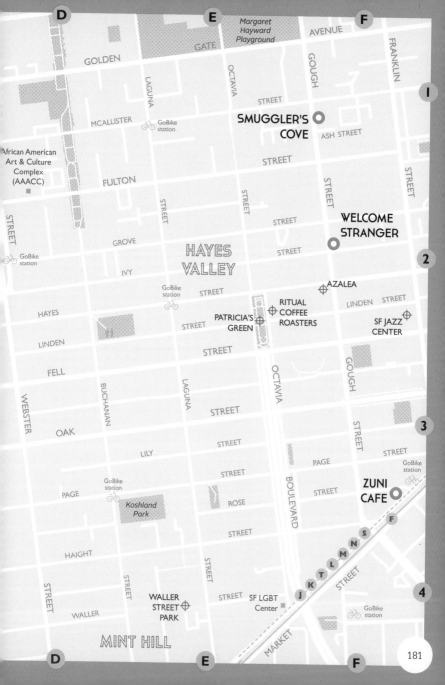

D

GOLDEN

E

GATE

Margaret
Hayward
Playground

AVENUE

F

FRANKLIN

I

MCALLISTER

GoBike
station

LAGUNA

OCTAVIA

STREET

GOUGH

SMUGGLER'S
COVE

ASH STREET

African American
Art & Culture
Complex
(AAACC)

STREET

FULTON

STREET

STREET

STREET

WELCOME
STRANGER

STREET

STREET

GoBike
station

GROVE

HAYES
VALLEY

STREET

2

IVY

GoBike
station

STREET

AZALEA

RITUAL
COFFEE
ROASTERS

LINDEN STREET

HAYES

STREET

PATRICIA'S
GREEN

SF JAZZ
CENTER

LINDEN

STREET

STREET

FELL

BUCHANAN

LAGUNA

OCTAVIA

GOUGH

STREET

WEBSTER

OAK

STREET

STREET

3

LILY

STREET

PAGE

STREET

PAGE

GoBike
station

GoBike
station

Koshland
Park

ROSE

BOULEVARD

STREET

ZUNI
CAFE

HAIGHT

STREET

STREET

F

S

N

M

WALLER
STREET
PARK

STREET

SF LGBT
Center

T

L

K

J

STREET

4

STREET

WALLER

MINT HILL

MARKET

STREET

GoBike
station

D

E

F

181

MAC'D

BROADWAY

LARKIN

PH

LEAVENWORTH

AVENUE

JONES

TAYLOR

I

VAN

POLK

STREET

PACIFIC

HYDE

POLK GULCH

STREET

JACKSON

PM PH

STREET

STREET

STREET

STREET

WASHINGTON

PM PH

STREET

STREET

NOB HILL

NESS

CLAY

STREET

STREET

BOB'S DONUTS AND PASTRIES

SACRAMENTO

STREET

GRACE CATHEDRAL

2

SWAN OYSTER DEPOT

CALIFORNIA

STREET

CALIFORNIA CABLE CAR

alifornia
'an Ness

STREET

PINE

STREET

FRANKLIN

AVENUE

THE GRUBSTAKE

BUSH

STREET

Mayflower Hotel

LOWER NOB HILL

Calista Organic Hotel

POLK

ALLIANCE FRANÇAISE DE SAN FRANCISCO

Mithila Hotel

HYDE

LEAVENWORTH

JONES

3

STREET

The Regency Ballroom

STREET

STREET

POST

LARKIN

STREET

STREET

STREET

TOMMY'S JOYNT

GEARY

WILSON & WILSON

STREET

STREET

O'FARRELL

STREET

STREET

STREET

4

ATHEDRAL HILL

Great American Music Hall

STREET

STREET

Tenderloin Museum

GoBike station

ELLIS

TENDERLOIN

D E F

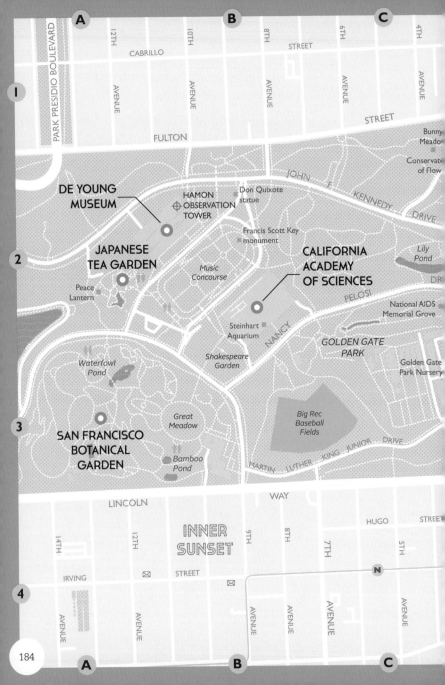

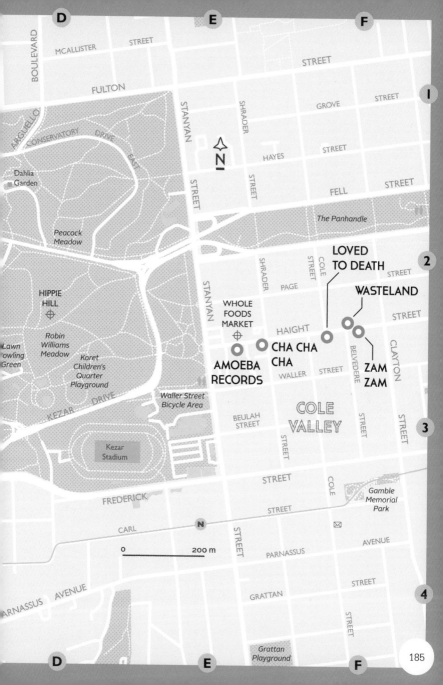

CORONA HEIGHTS

ROOSEVELT WAY

15TH STREET

Corona Heights Park

Randall Museum

STATES STREET

CASTRO STREET

15TH STREET

NOE STREET

GoBike station

SANCHEZ STREET

DUBOCE TRIANGLE

S
M
L
T
K
✉

16TH STREET

GoBike station

MARKET STREET

STREET

GoBike station

GILBERT BAKER MEMORIAL RAINBOW FLAG & CASTRO PRIDE FLAG POLE

Castro

17TH STREET

F

STREET

CASTRO

FORD STREET

TWIN PEAKS TAVERN

HARTFORD STREET

UNIONMADE WOMAN

UNIONMAD

UNIONMA

DOG EARED BOOKS

✉

18TH STREET

GLBT HISTORICAL SOCIETY

RAINBOW HONOR WALK

GoBike station

DOUGLAS STREET

EUREKA STREET

HARVEY MILK'S OLD CAMERA SHOP

STREET

19TH STREET

NOE STREET

ST

SANCHEZ

GoBike station

19TH STREET

DIAMOND STREET

STREET

STREET

Seward Mini Park

20TH STREET

CASTRO STREET

N

EUREKA VALLEY

STREET

21ST STREET

STREET

STREET

STREET

0   200 m

HILL STREET

STREET

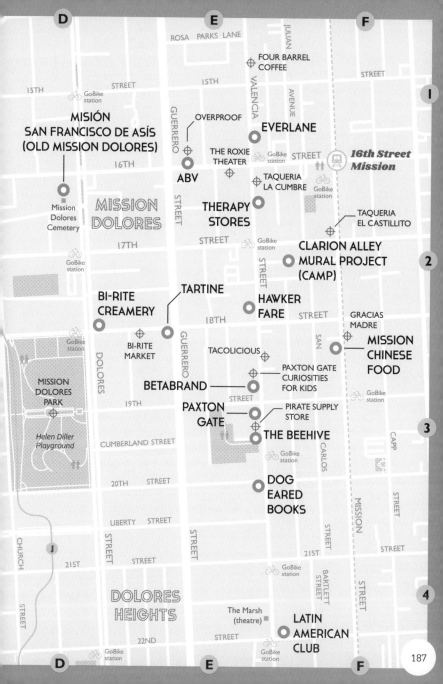

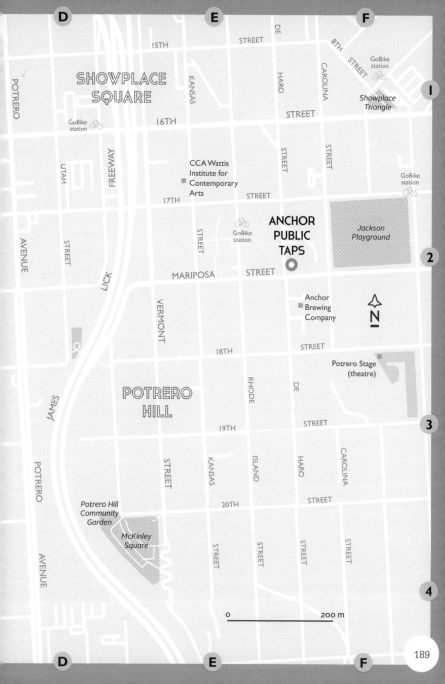

SHOWPLACE SQUARE

POTRERO HILL

15TH STREET
16TH
17TH
18TH
19TH
20TH
8TH STREET

POTRERO
UTAH
FREEWAY
LICK
VERMONT
JAMES
POTRERO AVENUE

KANSAS
HARO
CAROLINA
RHODE ISLAND
DE

GoBike station
GoBike station
GoBike station
GoBike station

Showplace Triangle

CCA Wattis Institute for Contemporary Arts

Jackson Playground

ANCHOR PUBLIC TAPS

MARIPOSA STREET

Anchor Brewing Company

N

Potrero Stage (theatre)

Potrero Hill Community Garden

McKinley Square

0   200 m

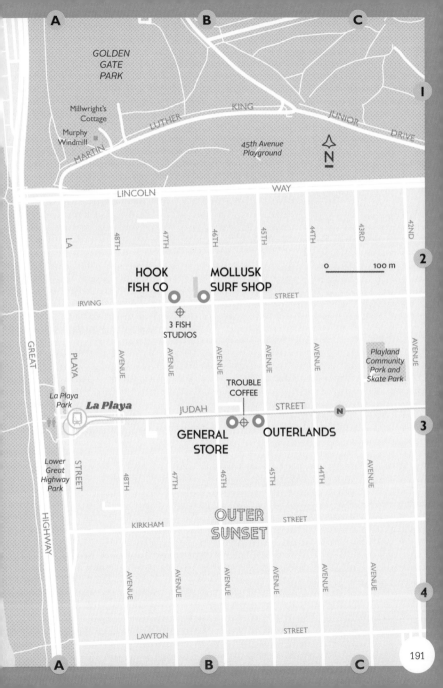

GOLDEN
GATE
PARK

Millwright's
Cottage

Murphy
Windmill

LUTHER

KING

JUNIOR

DRIVE

MARTIN

45th Avenue
Playground

N

1

LINCOLN

WAY

LA

48TH

47TH

46TH

45TH

44TH

43RD

42ND

2

0   100 m

HOOK
FISH CO

MOLLUSK
SURF SHOP

STREET

IRVING

3 FISH
STUDIOS

PLAYA

AVENUE

AVENUE

AVENUE

AVENUE

AVENUE

AVENUE

Playland
Community
Park and
Skate Park

GREAT

La Playa
Park

La Playa

JUDAH

TROUBLE
COFFEE

STREET

N

3

GENERAL
STORE

OUTERLANDS

Lower
Great
Highway
Park

STREET

48TH

47TH

46TH

45TH

44TH

AVENUE

KIRKHAM

STREET

OUTER
SUNSET

HIGHWAY

AVENUE

AVENUE

AVENUE

AVENUE

AVENUE

AVENUE

4

LAWTON

STREET

A

B

C

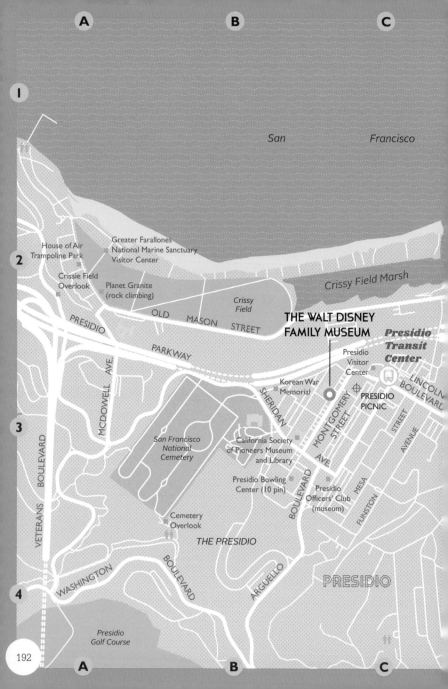

San   Francisco

House of Air
Trampoline Park

Greater Farallones
National Marine Sanctuary
Visitor Center

Crissie Field
Overlook

Planet Granite
(rock climbing)

PRESIDIO

Crissy Field Marsh

Crissy
Field

OLD   MASON   STREET

PARKWAY

THE WALT DISNEY
FAMILY MUSEUM

*Presidio
Transit
Center*

Presidio Visitor
Center

Korean War
Memorial

PRESIDIO
PICNIC

LINCOLN   BOULEVARD

MCDOWELL AVE.

SHERIDAN

MONTGOMERY STREET

STREET

AVENUE

San Francisco
National Cemetery

California Society
of Pioneers Museum
and Library

Presidio Bowling
Center (10 pin)

Presidio
Officers' Club
(museum)

BOULEVARD

MESA

FUNSTON

VETERANS   BOULEVARD

Cemetery
Overlook

THE PRESIDIO

ARGUELLO

PRESIDIO

WASHINGTON   BOULEVARD

Presidio
Golf Course

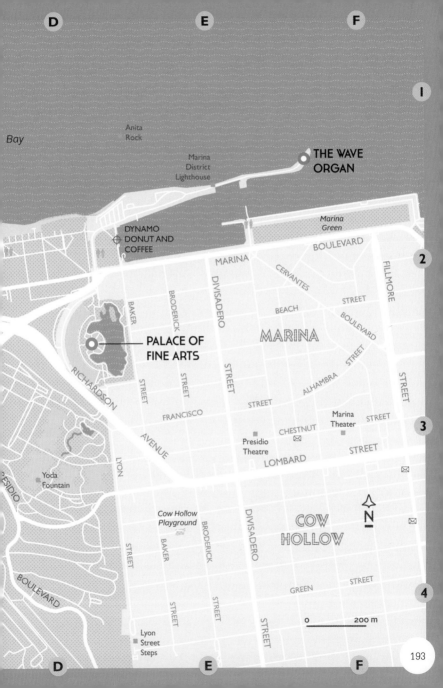

THE WAVE
ORGAN

Bay

Anita
Rock

Marina
District
Lighthouse

DYNAMO
DONUT AND
COFFEE

Marina
Green

BOULEVARD

MARINA

CERVANTES

STREET

DIVISADERO

BRODERICK

BAKER

BEACH

BOULEVARD

FILLMORE

PALACE OF
FINE ARTS

STREET

MARINA

STREET

ALHAMBRA

STREET

STREET

RICHARDSON

FRANCISCO

STREET

STREET

AVENUE

LYON

CHESTNUT

Presidio
Theatre

Marina
Theater

STREET

STREET

LOMBARD

STREET

Yoda
Fountain

PRESIDIO

Cow Hollow
Playground

BRODERICK

DIVISADERO

COW
HOLLOW

N

BAKER

STREET

BOULEVARD

STREET

STREET

STREET

STREET

GREEN

STREET

DIVISADERO

0   200 m

Lyon
Street
Steps

D

E

F

193

A NOTE FROM SAM

I particularly like guides – I like it when someone I meet at a bar scribbles five places down on a napkin for me to check out the next day. Connecting people with places and cataloguing it on paper seems like a comforting thought. I spent years making guidebooks for people that were new to cities for this reason. I always felt I wanted that little piece of what I loved to be handed onto someone who needed it and help them find where they fitted in a new and confusing place.

ABOUT THE AUTHOR

Sam Trezise has made a career around creating guidebooks, ever eager to introduce people to what truly makes a city great. He started his journey founding Insider Guides, a student-focused series to Australia and the UK.

In more recent times his attention has been on delving into the travel sector. Working with city councils, media providers and tourism commissions, he's been involved in projects of all shapes and sizes.

Over the past few years, he's divided his time living between San Francisco and Australia (with a few research trips in-between). During this period he has worked on producing Hardie Grant Travel's Half-Full Adventure Map Series. The locations he explored encompassed San Francisco, New York City, Tokyo, London and Melbourne. He has also written *Adelaide Pocket Precincts*.

ACKNOWLEDGEMENTS

Thanks so much to Melissa Kayser and Megan Cuthbert for commissioning this book and Hardie Grant for developing the ever useful Precinct series. I appreciated the chance to further explore this great city.

Without the top editing and pure patience of Alice Barker keeping my ramblings on track, this book certainly wouldn't have been as reader-friendly.

As a graphic designer by trade, I appreciate all of the hard work that goes into the layout, design and cartography. So thanks to Megan Ellis (typesetting), Michelle Mackintosh (design) and Emily Maffei and Jason Sankovic (cartography).

Cheers to all of the store owners, bartenders, baristas, servers and other staff who told me their stories and painted a picture of what the locations meant to them.

Cheers to locals, friends and family who spent time with me in the city and showed me what they loved about the place. Particular thanks to Joe, Maggie and Alex who contributed a lot. Thanks to my mother Lynne for hanging out in San Francisco a lot with me and my dad Greg for heading over a couple of times, too.

Thanks to Josh and Brenton for your support when I was back at home writing out the final pages.

PHOTO CREDITS

All images © Sam Trezise, except the following:

Page i Unsplash/James Ohlerking; 6 bottom Unsplash/David Castellon; 12–3 Unsplash/Brandon Nelson; 26–7, 137 bottom, 145 bottom, 149 top & bottom iStock Photo; 63 bottom, 152 top, 160 Alamy Images; 93 middle & bottom Unsplash/ Jake Weirick; 111 top Unsplash/Max Templeton; 130–1 Unsplash/Caleb Woods; 137 top & middle Shutterstock; 148 Unsplash/Jeremy Iwanga; 154–5 Unsplash/Aniket Deole; 157 top Unsplash/Angel Origgi; 157 middle Unsplash/ Michael Manns; 157 bottom Unsplash/Nathan Shipps; 158 Unsplash/Grant Porter; 159 top Unsplash/Aaron Thomas; 159 middle Unsplash/Chuck Grimmet; 159 bottom Unsplash/ Etienne Desclides; 161 top Unsplash/Denys Nevozhai; 161 bottom Unsplash/Milkovi; 196 second Unsplash/Chris Leipelt; 196 third, 197 second Unsplash/Josh Edgoose.

Published in 2019 by Hardie Grant Travel, a division of Hardie Grant Publishing

Hardie Grant Travel (Melbourne)
Building 1, 658 Church Street
Richmond, Victoria 3121

Hardie Grant Travel (Sydney)
Level 7, 45 Jones Street
Ultimo, NSW 2007

www.hardiegrant.com/au/travel

The maps in this publication incorporate data from:

© OpenStreetMap contributors
OpenStreetMap is made available under the Open Data Commons Open Database License (ODbL) by the OpenStreetMap Foundation (OSMF):
http://opendatacommons.org/licenses/odbl/1.0/. Any rights in individual contents of the database are licensed under the Database Contents License:
http://opendatacommons.org/licenses/dbcl/1.0/
Data extracts via Geofabrik GmbH
https://www.geofabrik.de
(c) Bay Area Motivate, LLC ("Motivate")
https://assets.fordgobike.com/data-license-agreement.html

A catalogue record for this book is available from the National Library of Australia

San Francisco Pocket Precincts
ISBN 9781741176315

10 9 8 7 6 5 4 3 2 1

Publisher
Melissa Kayser

Senior editor
Megan Cuthbert

Project editor
Alice Barker

Editorial assistance
Rosanna Dutson

Proofreader
Helena Holmgren

Cartographer
Jason Sankovic, Emily Maffei

Cartographic research
Claire Johnston

Design
Michelle Mackintosh

Typesetting
Megan Ellis

Index
Max McMaster

Prepress
Megan Ellis and Splitting Image Colour Studio

Printed and bound in China by LEO Paper Group